BEST EDITORIAL CARTOONS OF THE YEAR

JERRY GARDEN
Courtesy Garden ARToons

BEST EDITORIAL CARTOONS OF THE YEAR

2010 EDITION

Edited by
CHARLES BROOKS

PELICAN PUBLISHING COMPANY
GRETNA 2010

Library of Congress Serial Catalog Data

Best Editorial Cartoons, 1972-
Gretna [La.] Pelican Pub. Co.
v. 38 cm annual—
"A pictorial history of the year."

United States—Politics and Government—
1969—Caricatures and Cartoons—Periodicals.
E839.5.B45 320.9'7309240207 73-643645
ISSN 0091-2220 MARC-S

Printed in the United States of America
Published by Pelican Publishing Company, Inc.
1000 Burmaster Street, Gretna, Louisiana 70053

Contents

Award-Winning Cartoons

2009 PULITZER PRIZE

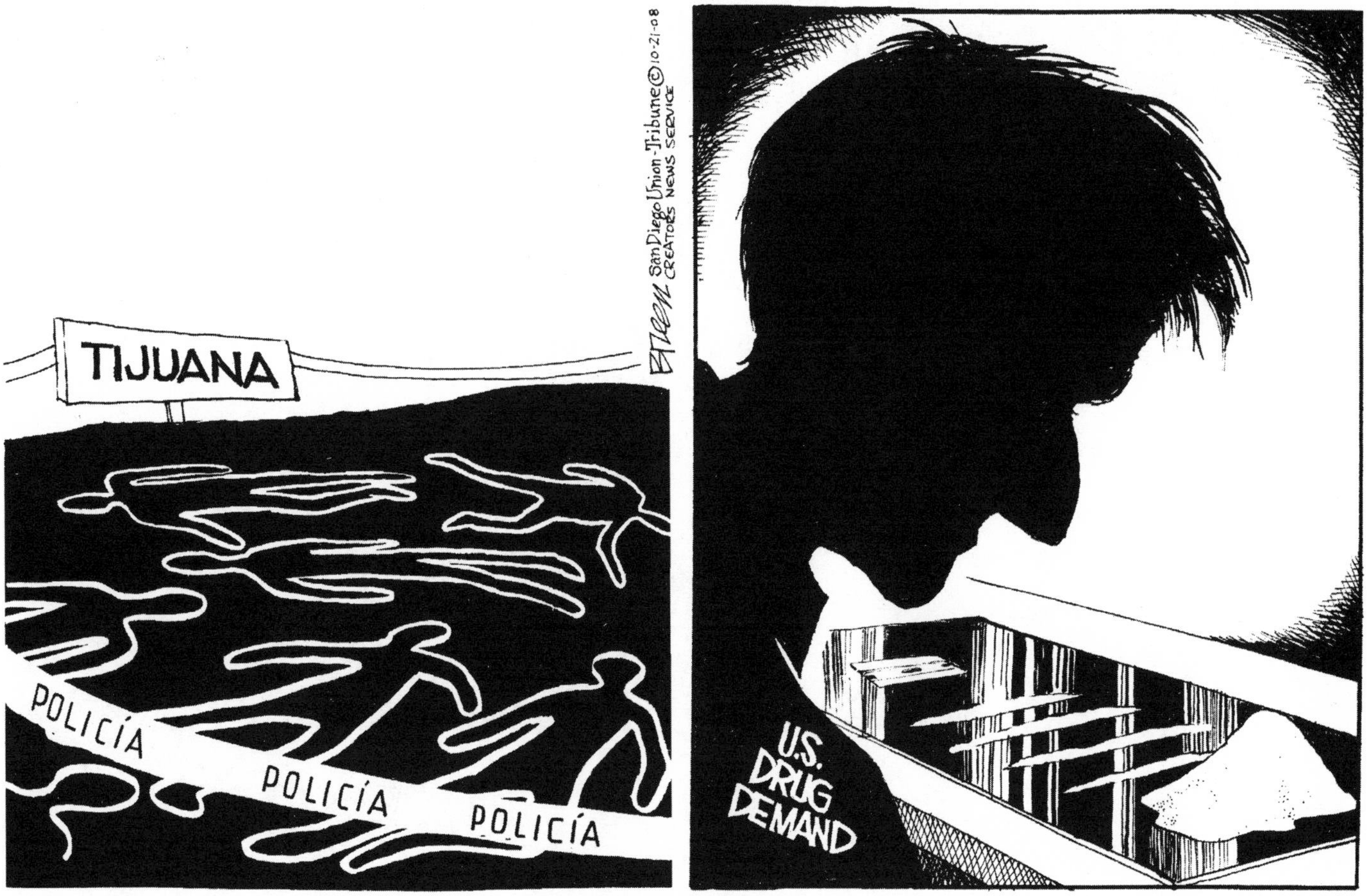

WHITE LINES

STEVE BREEN

Editorial Cartoonist
San Diego Tribune

Born in Los Angeles in 1970; attended the University of California at Riverside; editorial cartoonist for the *San Diego Tribune,* 2001 to the present; two-time winner of the Pulitzer Prize for editorial cartooning, having previously won the award in 1998; he is also the recipient of the 2009 National Headliner Award, the 2009 Overseas Press Club's Thomas Nast Award, and the National Press Foundation's 2007 Berryman Award; syndicated by Creators News Service; writes and illustrates books, among them *Stick* (2007), *Violet the Pilot* (2008), and *The Secret of Santa's Island* (2009).

2009 NATIONAL HEADLINER AWARD

STEVE BREEN

Editorial Cartoonist
San Diego Tribune

2009 THOMAS NAST AWARD

ETHANOL IS EXPENSIVE, IT DOES NOT REDUCE GREENHOUSE GASES AND IT CAUSES FOOD SHORTAGES.
WHO SAYS HE DOESN'T HAVE A BRAIN?
BREEN San Diego Union-Tribune © 5-13-08
COPLEY NEWS SERVICE

STEVE BREEN

Editorial Cartoonist
San Diego Tribune

2008 SIGMA DELTA CHI AWARD

(Awarded in 2009)

CHRIS BRITT

Editorial Cartoonist
State Journal-Register (Ill.)

Born in Phoenix, Arizona; editorial cartoonist for the Springfield, Illinois, *State Journal-Register;* previously worked for the *Arizona Business Gazette,* the *Sacramento Union,* the *Houston Post,* the Tacoma, Washington, *News Tribune,* and the *Seattle Times;* cartoons syndicated in more than 200 newspapers by Creators News Service; named Cartoonist of the Year in 1994 by the National Press Foundation; and in 2000 he was the only U.S. cartoonist to be recognized by the United Nations for cartoons dealing with peace in the Middle East.

2008 SCRIPPS HOWARD AWARD

(Awarded in 2009)

MIKE LUCKOVICH

Editorial Cartoonist
Atlanta Journal-Constitution

Born in Seattle, Washington, 1960; graduated from the University of Washington in 1982; served as editorial cartoonist at the *Greenville News* and the New Orleans *Times-Picayune* prior to joining the staff of the Atlanta *Journal-Constitution;* winner of the Pulitzer Prize in 1995, as well as the Reuben Award, the Thomas Nast Award, the National Headliner Award, and the Sigma Delta Chi Award.

2008 JOHN FISCHETTI AWARD

(Awarded in 2009)

LEE JUDGE

Editorial Cartoonist
Kansas City Star

Born in 1953; editorial cartoonist for the *Sacramento Union,* 1976-79, the *San Diego Union,* 1979-1980, and the *Kansas City Star,* 1980 to the present; previous winner of the Fischetti Award in 1982; served as president of the Association of American Editorial Cartoonists, 1989-90.

2009 HERBLOCK AWARD

PAT BAGLEY

Editorial Cartoonist
Salt Lake Tribune

Grew up in Southern California; began his editorial cartooning career in 1977; during a class at Brigham Young University, he sketched a cartoon; a few weeks later the cartoon was published in *Time* magazine; worked briefly as a caricaturist before being named editorial cartoonist for the *Salt Lake Tribune.*

BEST EDITORIAL CARTOONS OF THE YEAR

RUSSELL HODIN
Courtesy New Times (Calif.)

The Obama Administration

Barack Hussein Obama in January took office as the first black president of the United States. Although he faced a staggering economic crisis, the media hailed him as a new hope for real change. Many in the press were accused of losing their journalistic balance in their enthusiastic support for him. Candidate Obama promised to bring new openness to government, to reject congressional earmarks, and to close America's internment center at Guantanamo.

Within weeks, however, Congress had passed a monstrous earmark-laden spending bill and a stimulus package totaling trillions of dollars. Massive bailouts went to banks, lending institutions, and automakers.

Obama found it difficult to close Guantanamo and came under fire for allowing the Justice Department to investigate CIA methods of interrogation. The conflicts in Iraq and Afghanistan remained major challenges.

Obama chose universal health care as his top priority. Most insured Americans, however, expressed satisfaction with their medical coverage and opposed the government takeover of health care. As opposition to health care reform grew, Obama's personal approval ratings dipped below 50 percent.

TOM STIGLICH
Courtesy Northeast Times (Pa.)

Stiglich ©09
WWW.TOMSTIGLICH.COM
E
X P
E C T A
L O N G W A I
T B E F O R E S E E
I N G A D O C T O R
OBAMA CARE

WHILE ON VACATION OBAMA FINDS OTHER WAYS TO RESHAPE THE CONSTITUTION...
© 2009 Rob Smith Jr.com

ROB SMITH JR.
Courtesy DBR Media

MICHAEL RAMIREZ
Courtesy Investors Business Daily

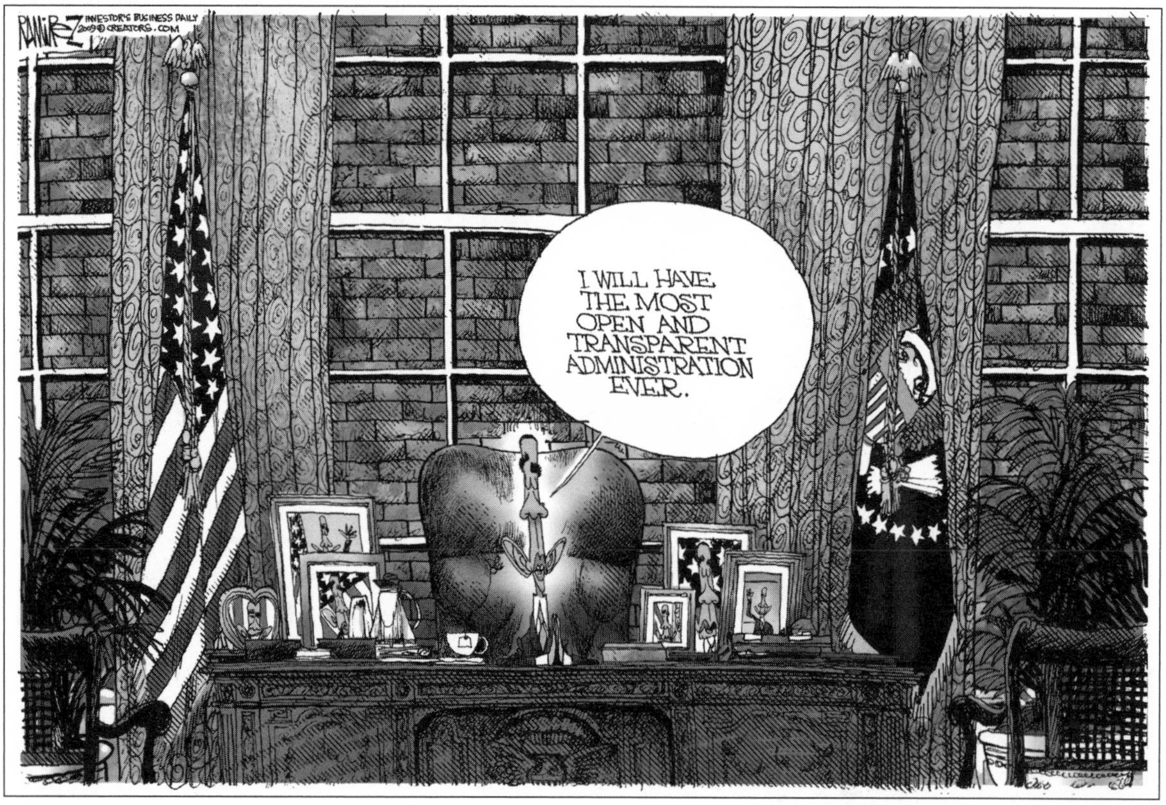
I WILL HAVE THE MOST OPEN AND TRANSPARENT ADMINISTRATION EVER.

DANA SUMMERS
Courtesy Orlando Sentinel

STEVE ARTLEY
Courtesy artleytoons.com

JAY LAMM
Courtesy Franklin Times

GLENN FODEN
Courtesy Artizans.com

JACKIE ROBINSON OF POLITICS
PRESS-REGISTER
CROWETOONS.com
Obama
44
BARACK OBAMA ELECTED NATION'S 44TH PRESIDENT

J.D. CROWE
Courtesy Mobile Press-Register

TIM JACKSON
Courtesy Chicago Defender

For decades, Americans of African descent have been relegated to the lowly task of cleaning up messes left behind by others.
THEN, BARACK OBAMA WAS ELECTED PRESIDENT OF THE UNITED STATES!
SOME THINGS NEVER CHANGE...
© Tim Jackson 2009 090115
DEFICIT
IRAQ
NO CHILD LEFT BEHIND
ECONOMY
KATRINA
JOBS LOST
TORTURE
BAIL OUTS
AFGHANISTAN
ABU GHRAIB
FORECLOSURES
Suggested by Lydia Janchitraponvej

ADVENTURES OF OBAMAMAN
The Somewhat Super Hero who Doesn't Save the Day But Partly Alleviates It
OBAMAMAN IS APPLYING HIS MEDICAL SKILLS TO AN ACCIDENT VICTIM WHEN HE GETS A CALL ABOUT AN URGENT CRISIS.
A BAND-AID? THIS MAN HAS BEEN DECAPITATED!
HOLY ECONOMIC MELTDOWN! I'M ON MY WAY!
EVENTUALLY
SORRY IT TOOK SO LONG TO GET HERE. I TOOK MASS TRANSIT.
HELP! THERE'S A $3 TRILLION "OUTPUT GAP" IN THE U.S. ECONOMY. WE COULD LOSE 20 MILLION JOBS!
THIS "PLAN" WILL ONLY FIX 1/5 OF THE PROBLEM.
NO NEED TO THANK ME. GOTTA GO! A METEOR HEADED TOWARD EARTH NEEDS TO BE SLIGHTLY SLOWED DOWN!
DIST. BY UNIVERSAL PRESS SYNDICATE RALL.COM
©2009 TED RALL

TED RALL
Courtesy Universal Press Syndicate

JEFF PARKER
Courtesy Florida Today

EXCITEMENT OVER BARACK OBAMA'S INAUGURATION CONTINUES TO BUILD...
THAT'S RIGHT, NATALIE. COME JANUARY 20TH, EXPECT: SIGNS IN THE HEAVENS; THE PARTING OF A SEA OF RED INK; HARMONY TO DESCEND ON WASHINGTON; PIGS WILL FLY!!...
I WORRY THE NATION'S EXPECTATIONS MIGHT BE SET JUST A TAD HIGH...
JEFF PARKER ©2009 FLORIDA TODAY
LIVE
HYPE NEWS
CAGLECARTOONS.COM

I KNEW MY HEALTH-CARE PLANS WOULD REDUCE COSTS...
WALT HANDELSMAN ©2009 Newsday
THESE ARE YOUR POLL NUMBERS...

WALT HANDELSMAN
Courtesy Newsday

BOB GORRELL
Courtesy Creators Syndicate

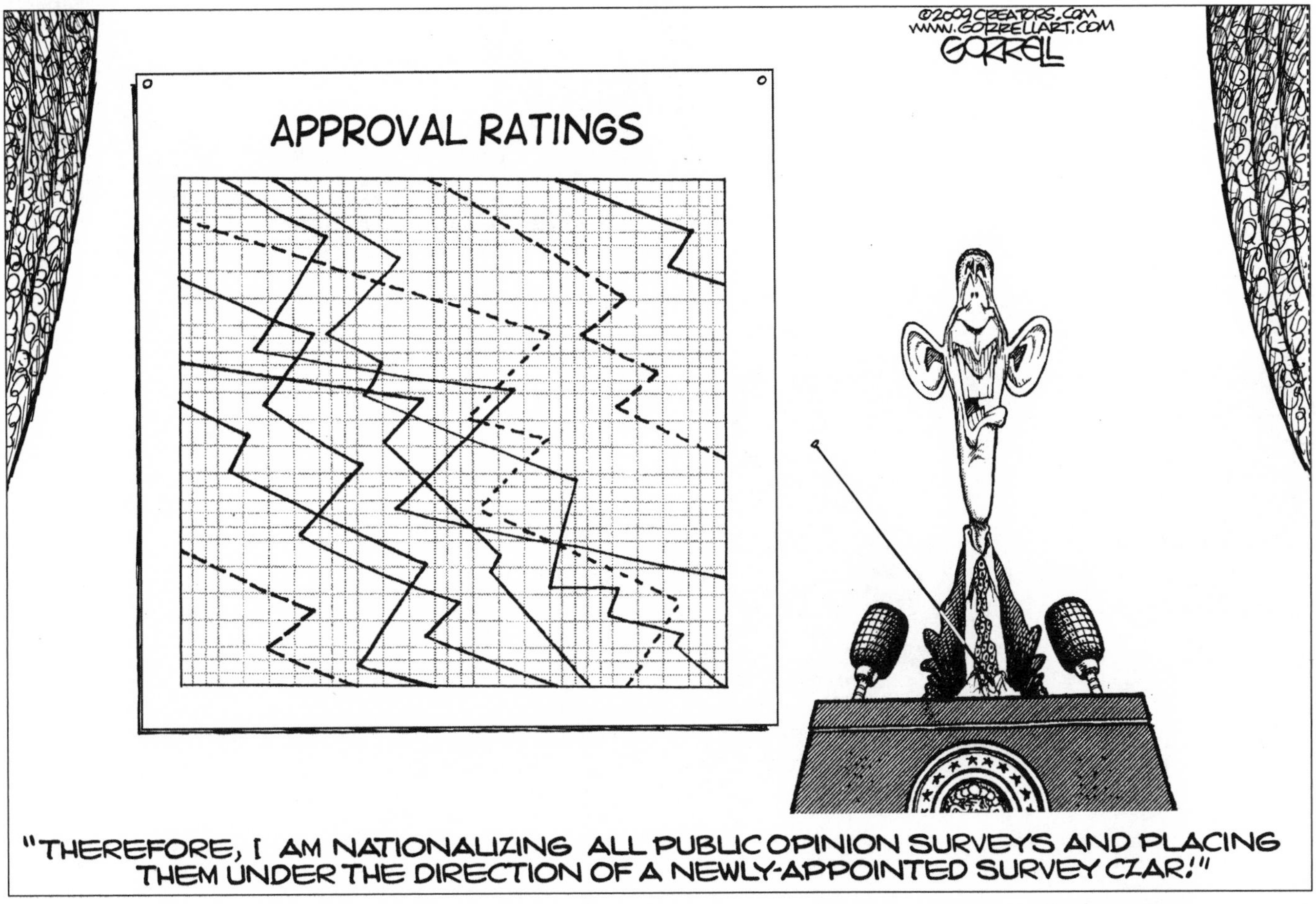
©2009 CREATORS.COM
WWW.GORRELLART.COM
GORRELL
APPROVAL RATINGS
"THEREFORE, I AM NATIONALIZING ALL PUBLIC OPINION SURVEYS AND PLACING THEM UNDER THE DIRECTION OF A NEWLY-APPOINTED SURVEY CZAR!"

artizans.com
YES WE CAN maybe...
ECONOMIC CALAMITY

JOHN LARTER
Courtesy Artizans.com

DAVID HITCH
Courtesy Worcester Telegram & Gazette (Mass.)

HITCH TELEGRAM & GAZETTE
I THINK I'D LIKE TO PHONE A CONSTITUTIONALIST....
THE OBAMA ADMINISTRATION THINKS 'RICH' PEOPLE...
A. SHOULD PAY FOR YOUR HEALTH CARE.
B. MUST SACRIFICE THEIR HARD-EARNED WAGES.
C. SHOULD HAVE THEIR SALARIES CAPPED.
D. WILL LEARN TO SHARE.
WHO IN THEIR RIGHT MIND WANTS TO BE A MILLIONAIRE?!?

LINDA BOILEAU
Courtesy Frankfort State Journal (Ky.)

POLITICAL REALITY
WARNING: WILL REMOVE PRESIDENTIAL SHINE WHEN USED WITH STIMULUS BILL
BOILEAU THE STATE JOURNAL 2009

DON'T WORRY, SIR... OPPONENTS OF YOUR HEALTH PLAN ARE JUST AN INSIGNIFICANT HANDFUL OF CRAZIES...
OBAMACARE
NO OBAMACARE
NO PUBLIC OPTION
NO SOCIALIZED MEDICINE
BREEN San Diego Union-Tribune 9-16 CREATORS.COM © 2009

STEVE BREEN
Courtesy San Diego Union-Tribune

MICHAEL RAMIREZ
Courtesy Investors Business Daily

RAMIREZ INVESTOR'S BUSINESS DAILY 2009 © CREATORS NEWS SERVICE
THE NUMBER OF PLANETS IN OUR SOLAR SYSTEM IS GOVERNMENT
HOW MANY STATES ARE THERE?
2+2= GOVERNMENT
1+1= GOVERNMENT
THE FIRST PRESIDENT OF THE UNITED STATES WAS GEORGE GOVERNMENT
A
10
-9
GOVERNMENT
6÷2=GOV
QUESTION: WHAT IS THE CAPITAL OF HAWAII?
ANSWER: GOVERNMENT
OBAMA
B
A=GOVERNMENT
B=GOVERNMENT
DEMOCRACY IS A FORM OF SOCIAL INEQUALITY
WHAT LANGUAGE DO AUSTRIANS
A YOUNG BARACK OBAMA.
WWW.IBDeditorials.com/cartoons

Tornoe
EDITOR & PUBLISHER
MEDIA

ROB TORNOE
Courtesy Editor & Publisher

HAP PITKIN
Courtesy Boulder Daily Camera

THE PRESIDENT ASKS WHAT HE NEEDS TO DO TO REGAIN HIS POPULARITY...
YOU NEED TO BRING THE MOON AND STARS DOWN FROM THE SKY, AND PUT THEM IN A "SPONGEBOB" LUNCH THERMOS.
OR - GET CONGRESS TO PASS HEALTH CARE REFORM.
HMMMM... HOW MANY STARS?
PITKIN '09 BOULDER CAMERA

MARSHALL RAMSEY
Courtesy Clarion Ledger

NATE BEELER
Courtesy Washington Examiner

MOU
TORONTO STAR
WELL, WELL,
DRINKING BEER IN PUBLIC.

THEO MOUDAKIS
Courtesy Toronto Star

JACK JURDEN
Courtesy Wilmington News-Journal

JACK JURDEN
WHERE'S BIDEN WHEN I NEED HIM?
HENRY LOUIS GATES AND CAMBRIDGE MASS. POLICE DEPT. REMARKS
NEWS JOURNAL DE.
I COULDN'T HAVE DONE BETTER MYSELF!
JOE

MIKE LESTER
Courtesy Rome News-Tribune (Ga.)

GARY VARVEL
Courtesy Indianapolis Star

I'M AN AGENT WITH THE INTERNAL REVENUE SERVICE. ACCORDING TO OUR RECORDS, YOU HAVEN'T BEEN PAYING YOUR TAXES.
OH, I WAS HOPING TO BE ON PRESIDENT OBAMA'S CABINET.
©2009 TIM HARTMAN

TIM HARTMAN
Courtesy Beaver County Times (Pa.)

ETTA HULME
Courtesy Fort Worth Star-Telegram

©2009 ETTATORIALS ETTA HULME
IF YOU DON'T MENTION IT, GEITHNER, THE COMMITTEE PROBABLY WON'T BRING IT UP
CONFIRMATION HEARING
SENATE FINANCE COMMITTEE
IOU IOU IOU IOU IOU
THE TREASURY SECRETARY NOMINEE WHO FAILED TO PAY TAXES

SO OBAMA'S GONNA CLOSE GUANTANAMO
IT'S NICE TO FINALLY HAVE A PRESIDENT WHO VALUES HUMAN LIVES
BRUBAKER
2009
MCT CAMPUS
KICK
WELL, MOST LIVES
cbrubaker@gmail.com

CHARLES BRUBAKER
Courtesy MCT Campus

ED STEIN
Courtesy Rocky Mountain News

GITMO
YEAH, I THOUGHT I'D BE GETTING OUT RIGHT AWAY, TOO.
edSTEIN '09 Nea
edSteinink.com

INVOKING THE SPIRIT OF FDR
©2009 TRIBUNE MEDIA SOUTH FLORIDA SUN-SENTINEL
LOWE 8-19
I PLEDGE YOU, PLEDGE MYSELF, TO A SO-SO NEW DEAL FOR THE AMERICAN PEOPLE!
HEALTH CARE REFORM

CHAN LOWE
Courtesy South Florida Sun-Sentinel

MR. PRESIDENT? THE JOINT CHIEFS ARE ON LINE ONE. SHALL I TELL THEM TO CALL BACK WHEN YOU ARE DONE WITH THAT OIL CHANGE?
SIGH...
GMC
JimBush jimbushart.com

JIM BUSH
Courtesy Providence Journal (R.I.)

REX BABIN
Courtesy Sacramento Bee

REXBABIN THE SACRAMENTO BEE
THE NEW NEW DEAL
STIMULUS

$1 TRILLION DEFICIT
OBAMA
AGENDA
THE TEAM IS GETTING A LITTLE FIDGETY, SIR!
7'09 CHUCK ASAY
COPYRIGHT 2009 CREATORS.COM

CHUCK ASAY
Courtesy Creators Syndicate

RICK MCKEE
Courtesy Augusta Chronicle

WHERE DID CAPTAIN OBAMA SAY HE WAS TAKING US?
SOMETHING ABOUT, "WHERE NO ONE HAS GONE BEFORE"...
$1.84 TRILLION DEFICIT
NCC-1701
R. MCKEE
©2009 THE AUGUSTA CHRONICLE 5/13

JOSEPH O'MAHONEY
Courtesy Patriot Ledger

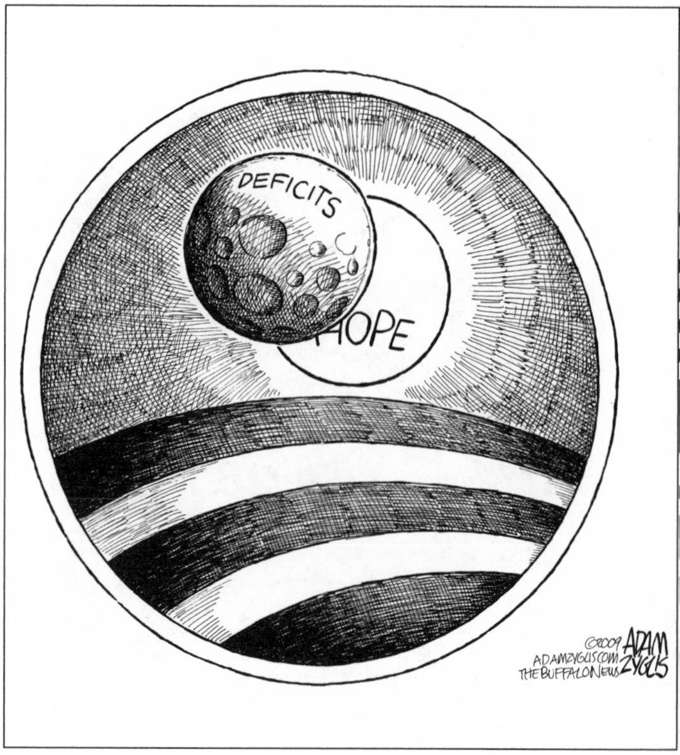

ADAM ZYGLIS
Courtesy Buffalo News

ROBERT ARIAIL
Courtesy robertariail.com

DAN FITZGERALD
Courtesy Courier-Journal (Ky.)

MARSHALL RAMSEY
Courtesy Clarion Ledger

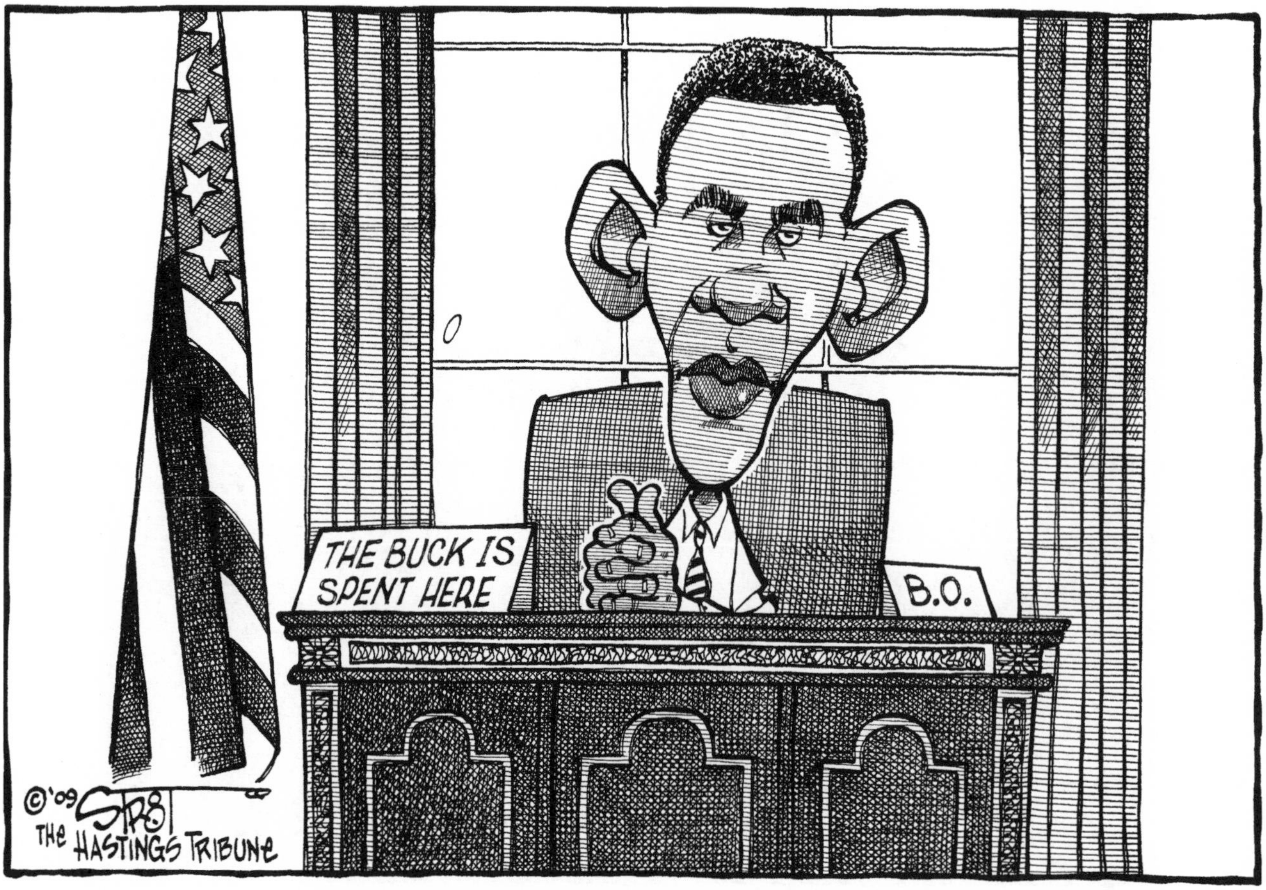
THE BUCK IS SPENT HERE
B.O.
©'09 STROOT
THE HASTINGS TRIBUNE

WAYNE STROOT
Courtesy Hastings Tribune (Neb.)

BOB GORRELL
Courtesy Creators Syndicate

The money you could be saving if Obama weren't president.
*APOLOGIES TO GEICO
©2009 CREATORS SYNDICATE INC.
WWW.GORRELLART.COM
GORRELL

FULLER© 2009
ARTIZANS.COM
I HAVE NO INTENTION OF RUNNING GENERAL MOTORS. NOW GET OUT. YOU'RE FIRED!
RICK WAGONER

JOHN FULLER
Courtesy Artizans.com

MIKE LESTER
Courtesy Rome News-Tribune (Ga.)

A nation trying to tax itself into prosperity is like a man standing in a bucket trying to lift himself up.
- Winston Churchill
CAN SOMEBEBODY GET RID OF THIS THING?
MIKE LESTER

CIA
HOLDER

JOE R. LANE
Courtesy EDITORIALCARTOONS.COM

CREATORS SYNDICATE
I SEE WHY DEMOCRATS DON'T MIND HIGH TAXES. THEY DON'T PAY THEM.
DAILY DONUT
TREASURY TAX CHEAT STILL IN
LIMO BOY OUT

CHIP BOK
Courtesy Creators Syndicate

SCOTT STANTIS
Courtesy USA Today

DEBT
CHAINS WE CAN BELIEVE IN...

SIR, DO YOU KNOW WHY I PULLED YOU OVER?
NO.
BUT I KNOW YOU ARE ACTING STUPIDLY.
GIVE IT A REST, BARACK.
POLICE
PR44BO
FOR AMERICANS FOR LIMITED GOVERNMENT
WILLIAM WARREN

WILLIAM WARREN
Courtesy Americans For Limited Government

BOB GORRELL
Courtesy Creators Syndicate

DUMB
IRAQ
DUMBER
AFGHANISTAN
GORRELL

MIKE LUCKOVICH
Courtesy Atlanta Journal-Constitution

NICK ANDERSON
Courtesy Houston Chronicle

TOWNS
LANDGREN

DON LANDGREN JR.
Courtesy The Landmark (Mass.)

RICK KOLLINGER
Courtesy Star-Democrat (Md.)

I'M BEING FOLLOWED
CIA
MY COVER'S BEEN BLOWN!
I'LL BE GIVEN A SHOW TRIAL AND MADE TO CONFESS
GEE.. I WONDER WHAT THAT WAS ALL ABOUT ?!?
AAAAARGH!
KOLLINGER

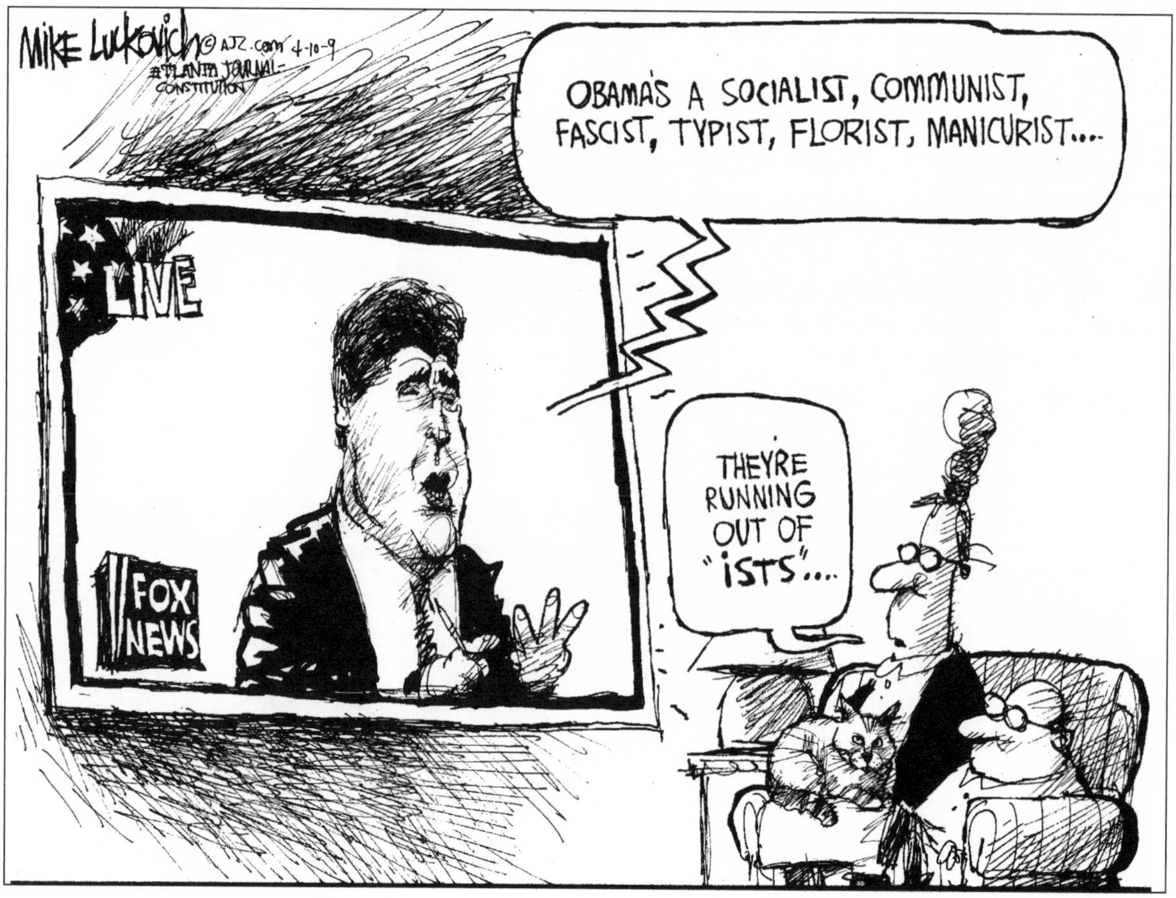
MIKE LUCKOVICH © AJC.com 4-10-9 ATLANTA JOURNAL-CONSTITUTION
OBAMA'S A SOCIALIST, COMMUNIST, FASCIST, TYPIST, FLORIST, MANICURIST....
LIVE
FOX NEWS
THEY'RE RUNNING OUT OF "ISTS"...

MIKE LUCKOVICH
Courtesy Atlanta Journal-Constitution

ED STEIN
Courtesy Rocky Mountain News

WE CAN STILL HAVE A CIVIL CONVERSATION IN THIS COUNTRY.
YOU LIE!
EDSTEIN '09 NEA
EDSTEININK.COM

Bailouts

With the nation's banking system threatening to collapse in 2008, former President George Bush began a series of government financial bailouts that ballooned ever higher. The bailouts, which initially focused on banks and lending institutions, later spread to include insurance giant AIG and the nation's automakers. General Motors and Chrysler found themselves compelled to receive huge federal loans and guarantees — and federal control.

To a large extent the auto industry brought the crisis upon itself. Unions demanded ever higher compensation packages, causing auto companies to go deeply into debt. As a result of the GM bailout, the government now owns about 45 percent of the company. Large banks were rescued with more billions after making risky home loans. Home prices crumbled and foreclosures mounted. Thousands of jobs disappeared.

A government plan to buy old cars, "clunkers," received good response but did not do much for the economy. It was feared that a federal takeover of the auto industry would meet similar problems experienced by Amtrak, Social Security, Medicare, Medicaid, Fannie Mae, Freddie Mac, and the U.S. Postal Service.

BRUCE MACKINNON
Courtesy Halifax Herald (Can.)

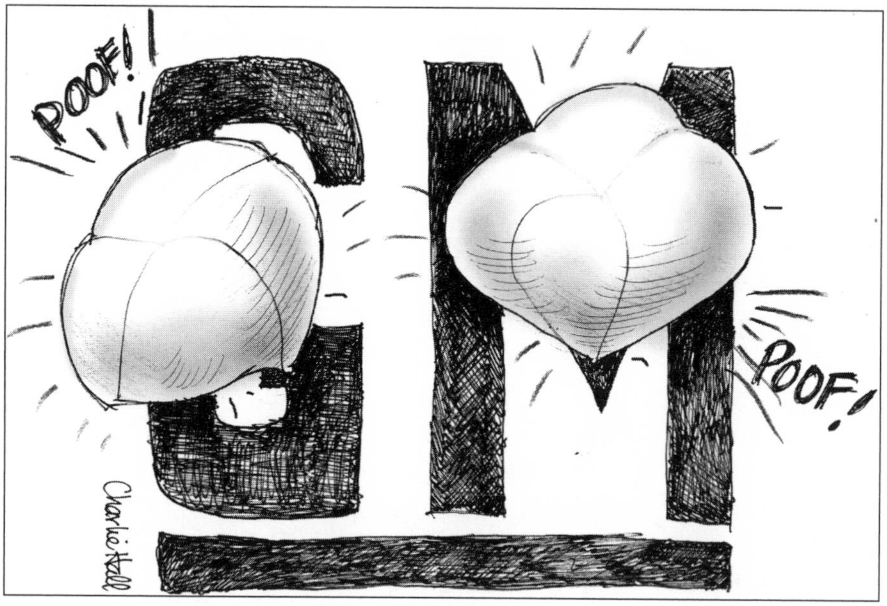
POOF!
POOF!

CHARLIE HALL
Courtesy Rhode Island News Group

I BOUGHT A HOUSE...
WITH A LOAN I COULDN'T AFFORD.
WHEN I STOPPED MAKING PAYMENTS...
THE BANK FORECLOSED.
BUT THANKS TO OBAMA...
I GET TO KEEP MY HOUSE...
WHILE TAXPAYERS PAY FOR IT!
I'M A SLUMDOG MILLIONAIRE!

TOM BECK
Courtesy Freeport Journal-Standard (Ill.)

MARTY RISKIN
Courtesy Penspeakcartoons.com

I NEED A QUICK QUALIFIER... DOES A DEADBEAT HUSBAND ON AN OLD RIDING MOWER MEET THE SPECIFICATIONS?
CASH FOR CLUNKERS PROGRAM

PHIL HANDS © THE TAMPA TRIBUNE 2008
WHY SHOULD MY TAX DOLLARS PAY TO BAILOUT MY IRRESPONSIBLE NEIGHBOR?
HOUSING RECOVERY PLAN
FORECLOSED
REDUCED
FOR SALE
HOME PRICES

PHIL HANDS
Courtesy Wisconsin State Journal

MIKE LUCKOVICH
Courtesy Atlanta Journal-Constitution

MIKE LUCKOVICH © AJC.COM 2-3-9
ATLANTA JOURNAL-CONSTITUTION
I BROUGHT CHAOS AND DESTRUCTION TO NEW YORK'S FINANCIAL DISTRICT....
I HEAR YOU GET A BONUS FOR THAT....

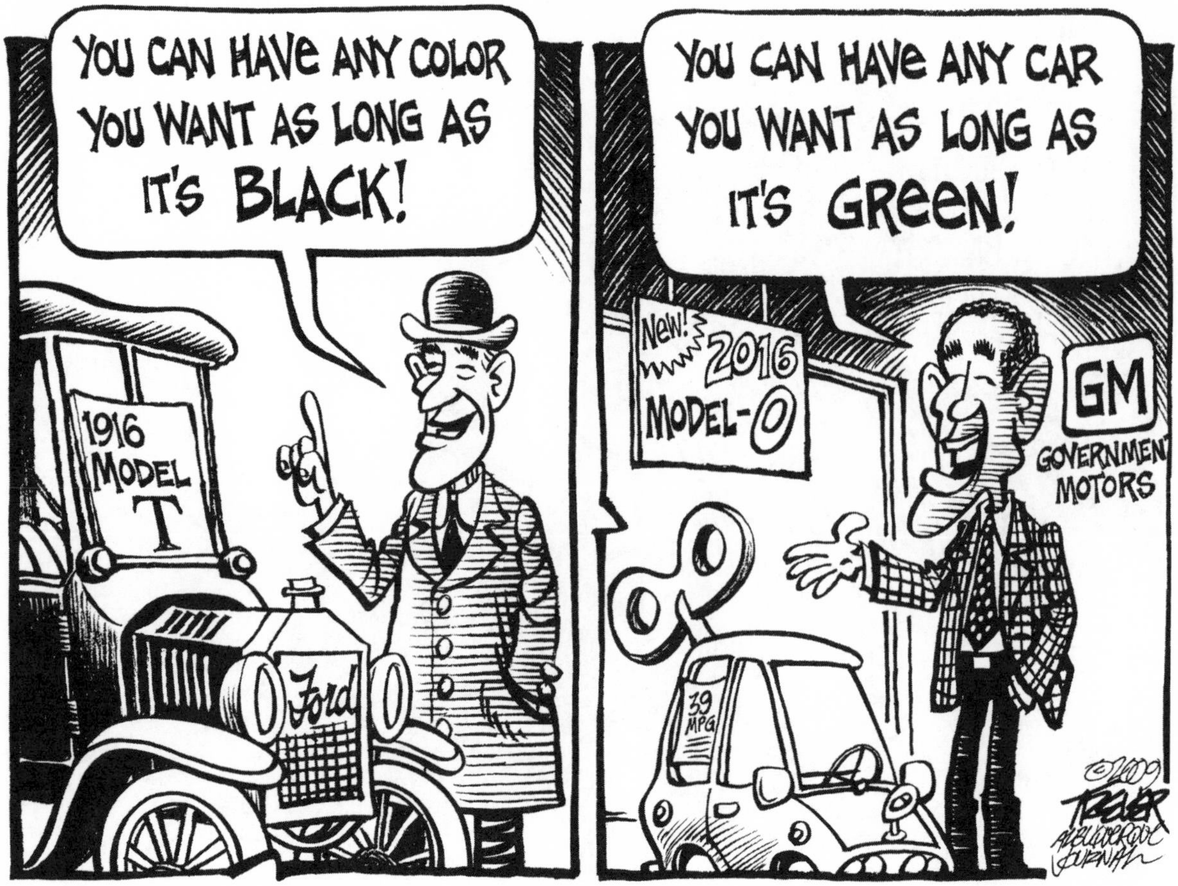
YOU CAN HAVE ANY COLOR YOU WANT AS LONG AS IT'S BLACK!
1916 MODEL T
Ford
YOU CAN HAVE ANY CAR YOU WANT AS LONG AS IT'S GREEN!
New! 2016 MODEL-O
GM
GOVERNMENT MOTORS
39 MPG
TREVER

JOHN TREVER
Courtesy Albuquerque Journal

MICHAEL RAMIREZ
Courtesy Investors Business Daily

RAMIREZ
INVESTOR'S BUSINESS DAILY
2008© CREATORS NEWS SERVICE
GIVE ME LIBERTY OR GIVE ME A GOVERNMENT BAILOUT.

©Lindstrom
DULUTH NEWS TRIBUNE 1-09
RISKY BORROWER
FOOLISH LENDER

STEVE LINDSTROM
Courtesy Duluth News-Tribune

TIM HARTMAN
Courtesy Beaver County Times (Pa.)

1971
WE'LL GIVE THIS A TRY, FOR A LITTLE WHILE, AND SEE IF IT WORKS.
AMTRAK
TIM HARTMAN
timhartman.com
30 YEARS (AND NOT ONE PENNY OF AMTRAK PROFIT) LATER
WE'LL GIVE THIS A TRY, FOR A LITTLE WHILE, AND SEE IF IT WORKS.
GM

O'MAHONEY
THE PATRIOT LEDGER
STIMULUS
BANKS
STIMULESS

JOSEPH O'MAHONEY
Courtesy Patriot Ledger

GM GETS BACK TO BASICS.
CURATOLO
WHAT'S IT GET PER GALLON?
GM

FRED CURATOLO
Courtesy Edmonton Sun

DANIEL FENECH
Courtesy Saline Reporter (Mich.)

Wall St.
DANIEL FENECH
©2009
WHATEVER YOU CAN GIVE... PLUS 10% GRATUITY

www.paulfellcartoons.com
GM
PAUL FELL ©2009
ARTIZANS SYNDICATE

PAUL FELL
Courtesy Artizans Syndicate

STEVE KELLEY
Courtesy The Times Picayune (La.)

THE TIMES · PICAYUNE © 2 0 0 9
S.KELLEY
RIDDLED WITH MISMANAGEMENT, BLOATED CONTRACTS AND WASTE... YOU NEED AN OVERHAUL!
GM
I'LL SEE THAT HE GETS ONE.
I WAS TALKING TO YOU.
GM

THE SACRAMENTO BEE REX BABIN
GM
UNDER NEW MANAGEMENT

REX BABIN
Courtesy Sacramento Bee

TIM HARTMAN
Courtesy Beaver County Times (Pa.)

I BOUGHT THIS AND I USED YOUR MONEY TO PAY FOR IT. AND TO MAKE SURE IT STAYS IN BUSINESS...
BUT I DON'T WANT IT.
TAX PAYERS
GM
...I'M FORCING THE FEDERAL GOVERMENT TO ONLY BUY CARS MADE BY IT. AND I'LL USE YOUR MONEY TO BUY THEM.
BUT I STILL DON'T WANT IT.
TAX PAYERS
GM
timhartman.com ©2009
TIMHARTMAN

VIC HARVILLE
Courtesy Stephens Media

J.D. CROWE
Courtesy Mobile Press-Register

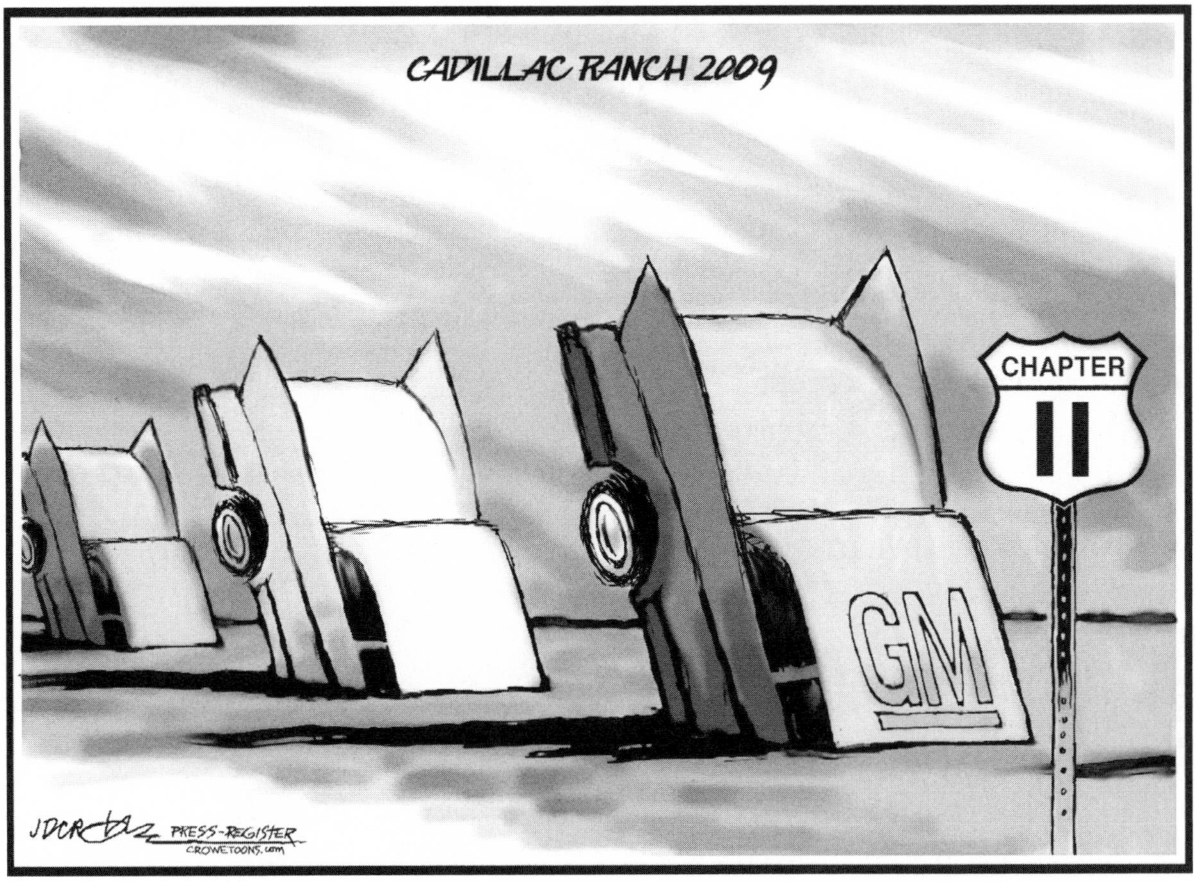

Facelift..new body parts...
but, he still left me for
this younger model...
Clunker
2009
The News

ANNETTE BALESTERI
Courtesy Antioch News (Calif.)

It's Only For
CARS!
Lompoc Record
CASH FOR CLUNKERS
Carlson/Smith "Dr.Draw"
2009 Lompoc Record

BILL SMITH and LYNN CARLSON
Courtesy Lompoc Record

STEVE KELLEY
Courtesy The Times Picayune (La.)

THE TIMES-PICAYUNE
© 2009
HOW MUCH CAN I GET
FOR MY WORN OUT,
UNRELIABLE GUZZLER?
CASH
FOR
CLUNKERS

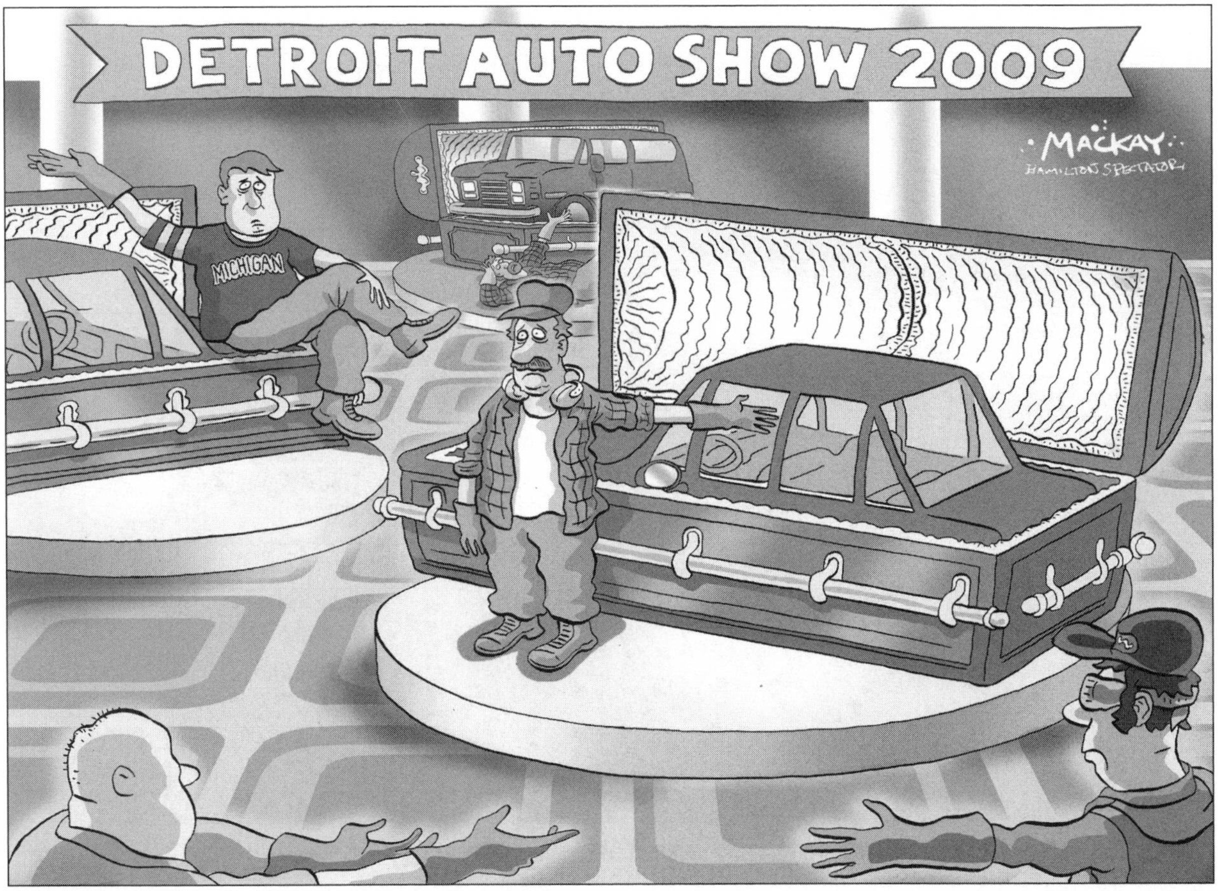
DETROIT AUTO SHOW 2009
MACKAY
HAMILTON SPECTATOR
MICHIGAN

GRAEME MACKAY
Courtesy Hamilton Spectator (Can.)

RICK MCKEE
Courtesy Augusta Chronicle

WOULD YOU RELAX? ...ANY MINUTE NOW SOME GUY IS GONNA POP OUT and YELL "APRIL FOOL!"
AUTO INDUSTRY
GOVERNMENT TAKEOVER
The AUGUSTA CHRONICLE ©2009

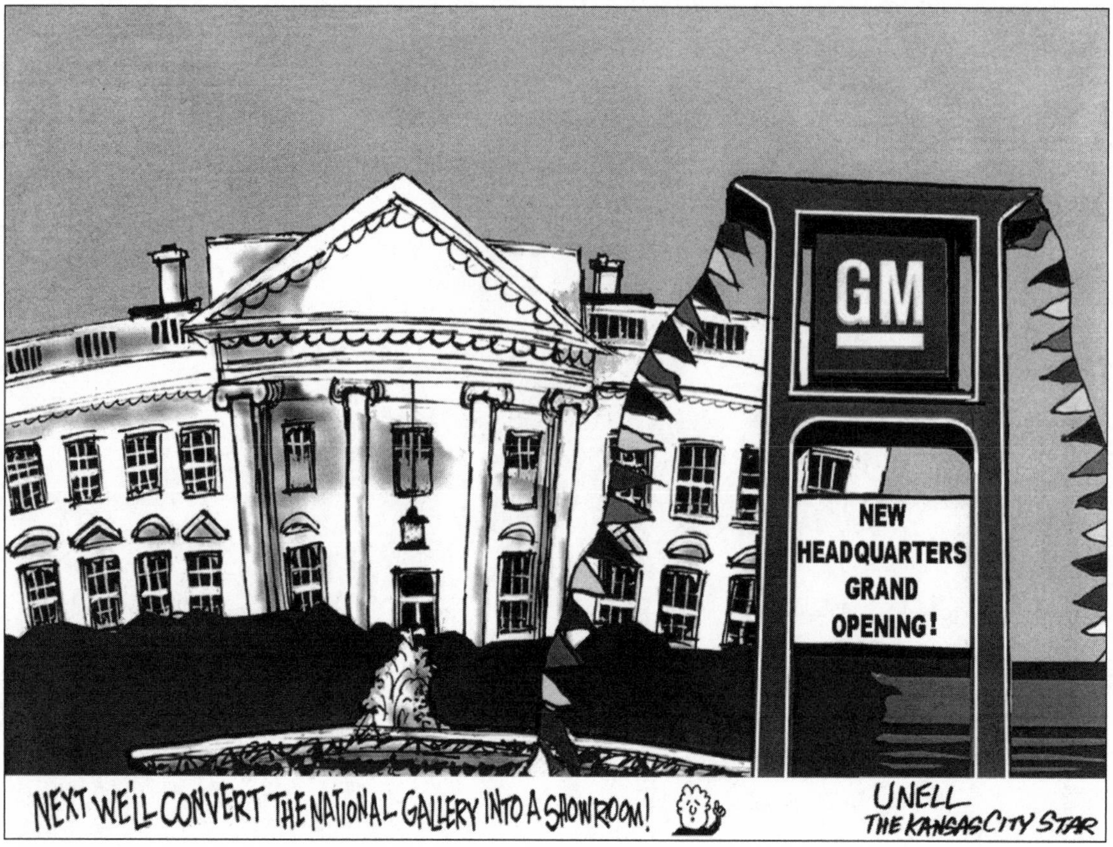

ROBERT UNELL
Courtesy Kansas City Star

PHIL HANDS
Courtesy Wisconsin State Journal

COME ON! FILL 'ER UP. WE'RE NEARLY THERE.
ULP.
AUTO INDUSTRY
UNION
FITZSIMMONS ©
THE ARIZONA DAILY STAR '09
CAGLECARTOONS.COM

DAVID FITZSIMMONS
Courtesy Arizona Daily Star

JEFF KOTERBA
Courtesy Omaha World-Herald

GOVERNMENT FINANCIAL RESCUE PLANS ARE LIKE A BOX OF CHOCOLATES... YOU NEVER KNOW WHAT YOU'RE GONNA GET.
Geithner's
KOTERBA
OMAHA WORLD-HERALD

MICHAEL RAMIREZ
Courtesy Investors Business Daily

SCOTT STANTIS
Courtesy USA Today

Congress

Congress struggled throughout the summer to pass controversial health care reform, but mounting public opposition pushed a self-imposed deadline further and further back. Critics accused Congress of trying to foist a system on the public that they themselves would not be subject to. Congressmen going home to town hall meetings faced angry constituents upset with the Democratic plan. Some congressmen ducked the town hall meetings altogether.

House Speaker Nancy Pelosi came under fire when she accused the CIA of having lied to Congress about its use of enhanced interrogation techniques against suspected terrorists.

Sonia Sotomayor was sworn in as the U.S. Supreme Court's first Hispanic justice. Conservative Republicans offered only nominal resistance to her nomination. Critics cited her decision denying white firefighters' claims of racial discrimination. Sotomayor was also criticized for her statements that public policy was determined by the courts, and that she, as a "wise Latina," would reach better decisions than a white male.

Following government bailouts, some lawmakers slammed auto executives for receiving bonuses and being out of touch with consumers' needs.

BILL GARNER
Courtesy Creators Syndicate

I'M AFRAID YOU'VE MISCONSTRUED MY STATEMENT...
YOU STUPID CRACKER...
©2009 ARTIZANS.com
HALL

ED HALL
Courtesy Baker County Press (Fla.)

IT'S THE TAX MONEY WE COULD HAVE BEEN SAVING...
if we hadn't spent like drunken sailors during the fat years —
EVANS ©'09

PETER EVANS
Courtesy Islander News (Fla.)

BRUCE BEATTIE
Courtesy Daytona Beach News-Journal

BEATTIE
....AND DO YOU PROMISE NOT TO HAVE AN AFFAIR, CALL A HOOKER, STASH $90 GRAND IN A FREEZER, SELL ANY SENATE SEATS, DISAPPEAR FOR A WEEK, TAP YOUR FOOT IN AN AIRPORT RESTROOM....

Amended Oath of Office

CONGRESS
"I SAID YOU'D GET COVERAGE. I DIDN'T SAY IT WOULD BE THE SAME AS MINE."
KOLLINGER

RICK KOLLINGER
Courtesy Star-Democrat (Md.)

DICK LOCHER
Courtesy Chicago Tribune

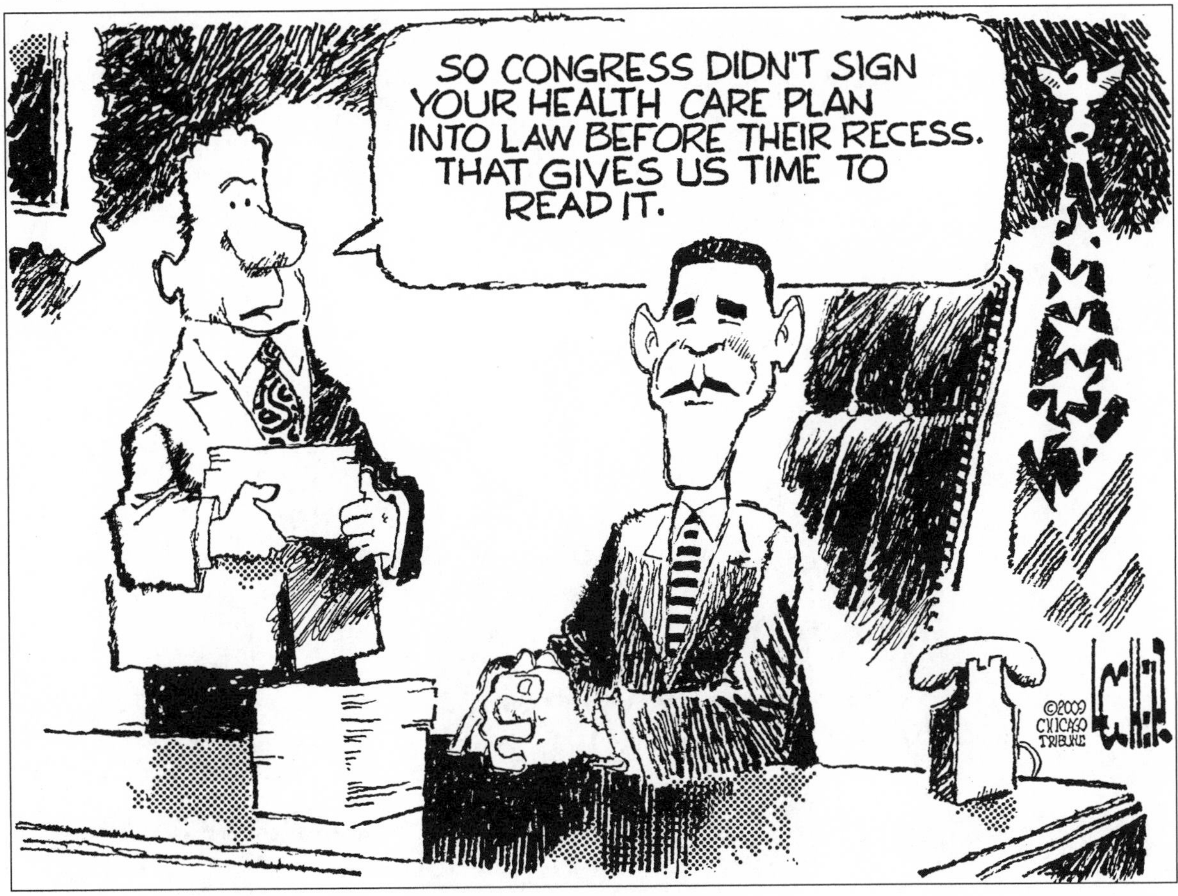

SO CONGRESS DIDN'T SIGN YOUR HEALTH CARE PLAN INTO LAW BEFORE THEIR RECESS. THAT GIVES US TIME TO READ IT.
©2009 CHICAGO TRIBUNE

It's not swine flu...
IT'S the H1N1 virus you idiots!
Folks are giving PORK a bad rap!
I agree.
CONGRESS

DEB MILBRATH
Courtesy CNN AAEC

BOB LANG
Courtesy rightoons.com

LANG © 2009 RighToons.com
HOW WAS YOUR SUMMER VACATION?
WHAT ARE YOU...SOME KIND OF @*★ SADIST?
TAR
HEALTH CARE TOWN HALL REPORTS
PLEASE WIPE YOUR FEET!
CONGRESS

THERE.. THERE CONGRESSMAN
SOB IT WAS AWFUL... ALL THOSE PEOPLE ASKING QUESTIONS!
YOU'RE BACK IN D.C. NOW.. NO ONE WILL QUESTION YOU.
CONGRESSMAN GROPE
PRIVATE
CONGRESS RETURNS FROM RECESS
KOLLINGER

RICK KOLLINGER
Courtesy Star-Democrat (Md.)

PETER DUNLAP-SHOHL
Courtesy Anchorage Daily News

DOWN, ROLL OVER, PLAY DEAD, BEG...
BIG PHARMA
DUNLAP-SHOHL
NOT ONLY DOES CONGRESS ENJOY A GREAT HEALTH PLAN.
THEY EVEN HAVE A FULL-TIME PERSONAL TRAINER

REVENUE
GOVT. SPENDING APPETITE

PETER EVANS
Courtesy Islander News (Fla.)

YER BLOATED, OVER-EXTENDED AND OUT OF TOUCH!
Ford
GM

ED HALL
Courtesy Baker County Press (Fla.)

BOB GORRELL
Courtesy Creators Syndicate

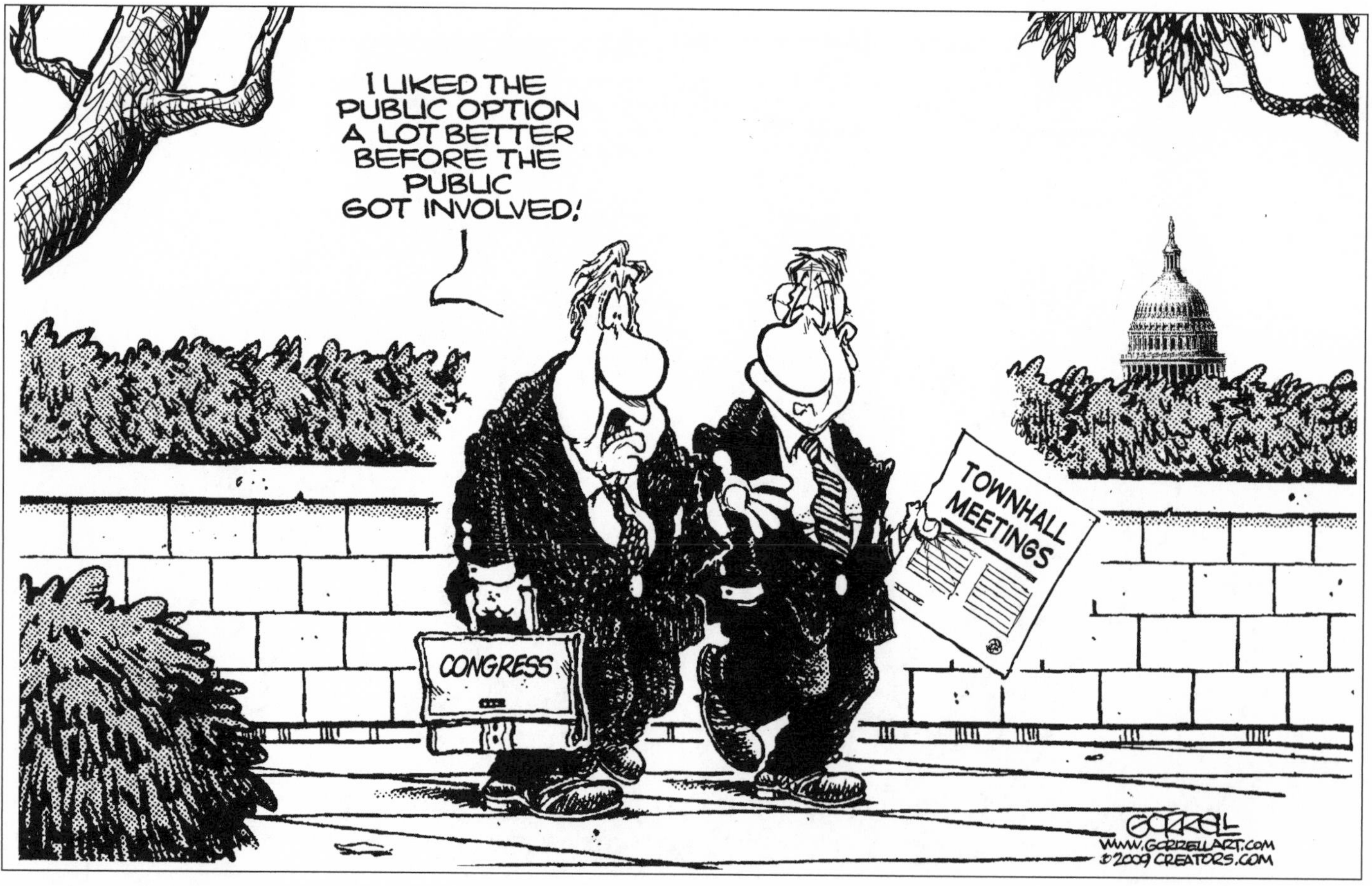
I LIKED THE PUBLIC OPTION A LOT BETTER BEFORE THE PUBLIC GOT INVOLVED!
CONGRESS
TOWNHALL MEETINGS
GORRELL
WWW.GORRELLART.COM
©2009 CREATORS.COM

I'M T. BOONE PICKENS, HERE IN THE HALLS OF CONGRESS - ALSO KNOWN AS THE SAUDI ARABIA OF WIND - TO PROMOTE HOT AIR AS A SUSTAINABLE SOURCE OF ENERGY...
ACME WIND POWER GENERATOR
HTTP://STEVE-RUSTAD.PETALUMA360.COM

STEVE RUSTAD
Courtesy petaluma360.com

TIM HARTMAN
Courtesy Beaver County Times (Pa.)

WHEN WE CLOSE GITMO, THE PRISONERS CAN COME TO JOHNSTOWN. IN FACT, THEY CAN LIVE WITH ME!
JOHN MURTHA
TIM HARTMAN ©2009
WE'LL WAIT UNTIL AMERICAN IDOL IS DONE, THEN WE'LL KILL HIM.

EDSTEIN '09 Nea
EDSTEININK.COM
YOU HAVE THE AUDACITY TO COME TO US WITH A PRE-EXISTING CONDITION?
LIFE AIN'T FAIR HEALTH INSURANCE CO.
DEATH PANEL

ED STEIN
Courtesy Rocky Mountain News

MIKE KEEFE
Courtesy Denver Post

MikeKeefe THE DENVER POST 8-21-09
WHY AREN'T WE USING THE HIGHWAY?
I DON'T BELIEVE IN PUBLIC OPTIONS!
U.S. I-70

Health/Education

President Obama and Democrats in Congress pushed hard for nationalized health care. Many fear government-run health care will mean long waiting lines for treatment, as in Great Britain and Canada. Universal health care would add millions of people to insurance rolls, without increasing the numbers of medical personnel. Many believe that will lead to rationing of medical treatment.

Former Alaska Gov. Sarah Palin suggested that the health care reform bill would set up "death panels" charged with making decisions on end of life care. Another worry about health care reform is cost. Critics say the cost of health care would increase dramatically after the government takes control. Obama has contended that getting rid of waste, fraud, and abuse would pay for the additional cost of universal health care, a claim rejected by Washington insiders. A new strain of influenza in Mexico, officially named H1N1 but dubbed swine flu, rapidly spread worldwide, causing a shocking number of deaths.

Obama made a controversial televised speech to school children, urging them to stay in school and study hard. Roughly half of the three million people who start college each year reportedly drop out before they earn their degrees.

STEPHEN TEMPLETON
Courtesy Flathead Beacon

STEVE LINDSTROM
Courtesy Duluth News-Tribune

RICK KOLLINGER
Courtesy Star-Democrat (Md.)

I'LL LET YOU FILL IN THE DETAILS- JUST BE QUICK ABOUT IT!
UNIVERSAL HEALTH CARE by B. OBAMA
CONGRESS
©2009 TREVER ALBUQUERQUE JOURNAL

JOHN TREVER
Courtesy Albuquerque Journal

WILLIAM WARREN
Courtesy Americans For Limited Government

IT'S SLIPPING FAST!
WE NEED AN EMERGENCY OPERATION, NOW!
THAT'LL BE A 7-MONTH WAIT...
PUBLIC SUPPORT FOR OBAMA-CARE
©2009 WILLIAM WARREN FOR AMERICANS FOR LIMITED GOVERNMENT

What do you want? To be taken to our leader?
No, free health care.
Charlie Hall

CHARLIE HALL
Courtesy Rhode Island News Group

OUR INSURANCE COMPANY IS CLAIMING IT WAS A PRE-EXISTING CONDITION!!
Hunau 09

TONY BAYER
Courtesy News-Dispatch (Ind.)

BARRY HUNAU
Courtesy cartoonsbybarry.com

HELPING THE NEEDY IS COMMUNISM! NO GOV'T HEALTH CARE!
Let the uninsured die or go bankrupt... JUST DON'T RAISE TAXES!
HELP!
uninsured
Bayer ©'09
tonybayertoons.com

ISN'T THAT MY PURSE?
HEALTH CARE BIZ.
©2009 ADAMZYGLIS.COM THE BUFFALONEWS
ADAM ZYGLIS

ADAM ZYGLIS
Courtesy Buffalo News

BOB LANG
Courtesy rightoons.com

LANG © 2009 RighToons.com
LET ME LOOK AT YOUR FOOT...
YOUR THROAT LOOKS SORE- I REALLY SHOULD LOOK AT THAT!
HOLD STILL-THIS WON'T HURT A BIT!
OH THANK YOU, PRESIDENT OBAMA FOR SAVING ME FROM THESE HOOLIGANS!
OBAMA FACTS:
GANGS OF GREEDY DOCTORS ARE ROAMING THE STREETS OF AMERICA, REMOVING THE FEET AND TONSILS OF UNSUSPECTING CITIZENS FOR OUTRAGEOUS PROFITS....

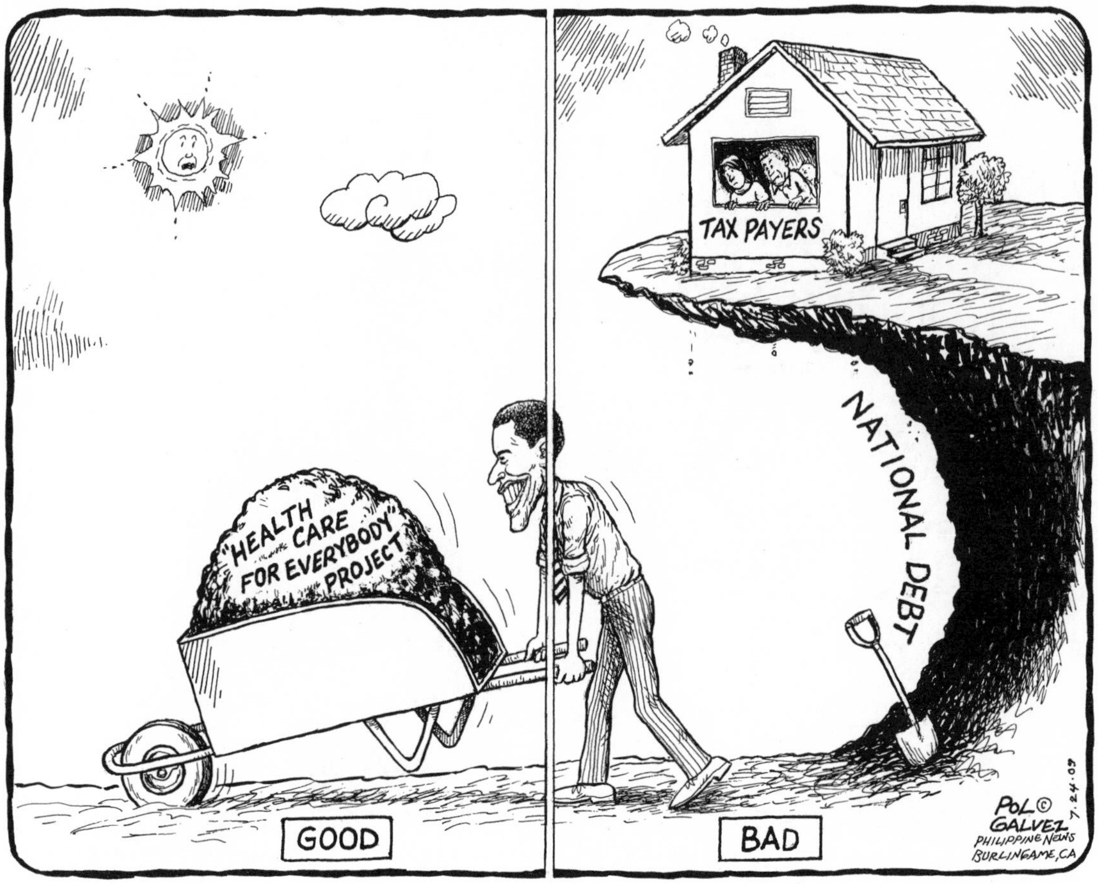

POL GALVEZ
Courtesy Philippine News

STEVE MCBRIDE
Courtesy The Reporter (Kan.)

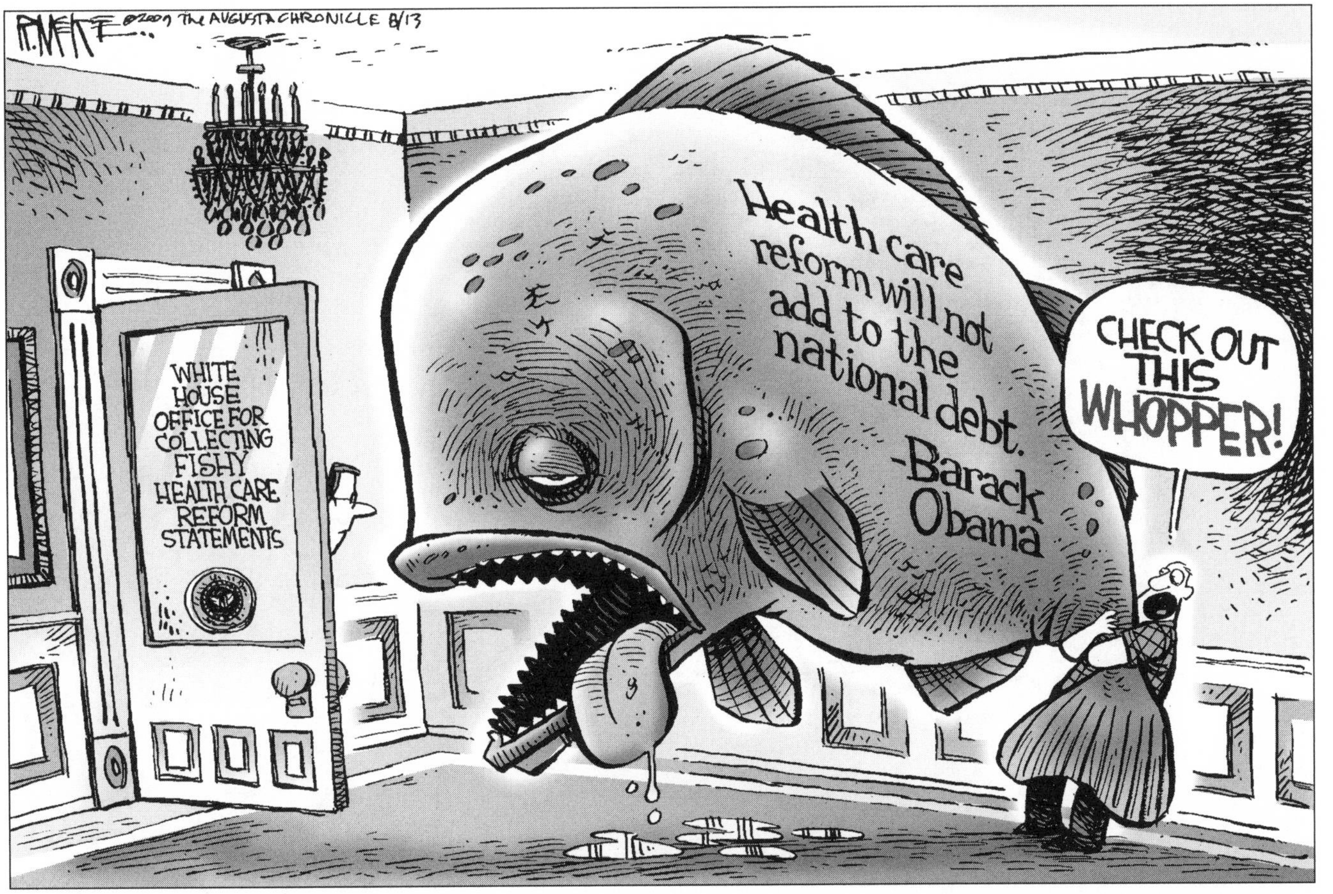
©2009 The Augusta Chronicle 8/13
Health care reform will not add to the national debt. -Barack Obama
CHECK OUT THIS WHOPPER!
WHITE HOUSE OFFICE FOR COLLECTING FISHY HEALTH CARE REFORM STATEMENTS

RICK MCKEE
Courtesy Augusta Chronicle

KEVIN KALLAUGHER (KAL)
Courtesy The Economist,
Kaltoons.com

EXCUSE ME! CAN ANYONE TELL ME IF THIS IS THE PATH TO COMPREHENSIVE AND AFFORDABLE HEALTH CARE?
SPECIAL INTERESTS
WE WELCOME YOUR PROPOSALS
KAL 2009 The Economist

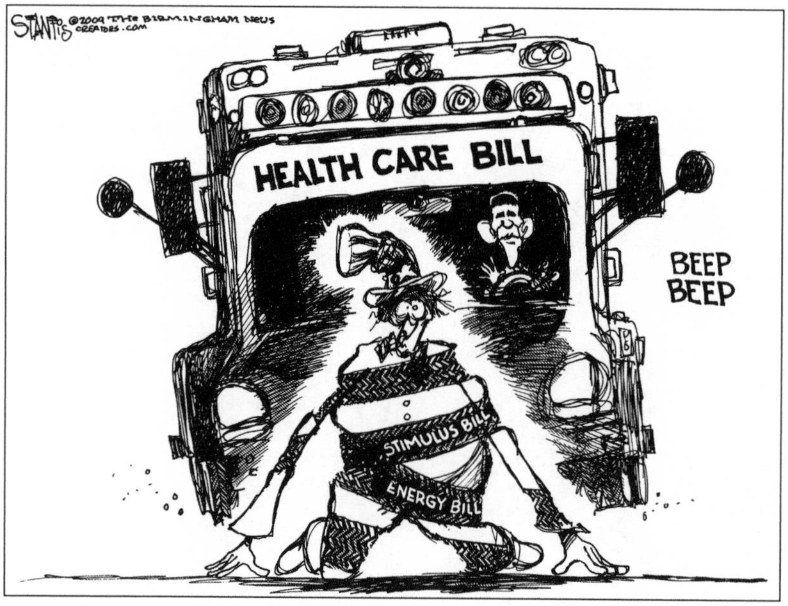

SCOTT STANTIS
Courtesy Birmingham News

JIM BUSH
Courtesy Providence Journal (R.I.)

WAYNE STROOT
Courtesy Hastings Tribune (Neb.)

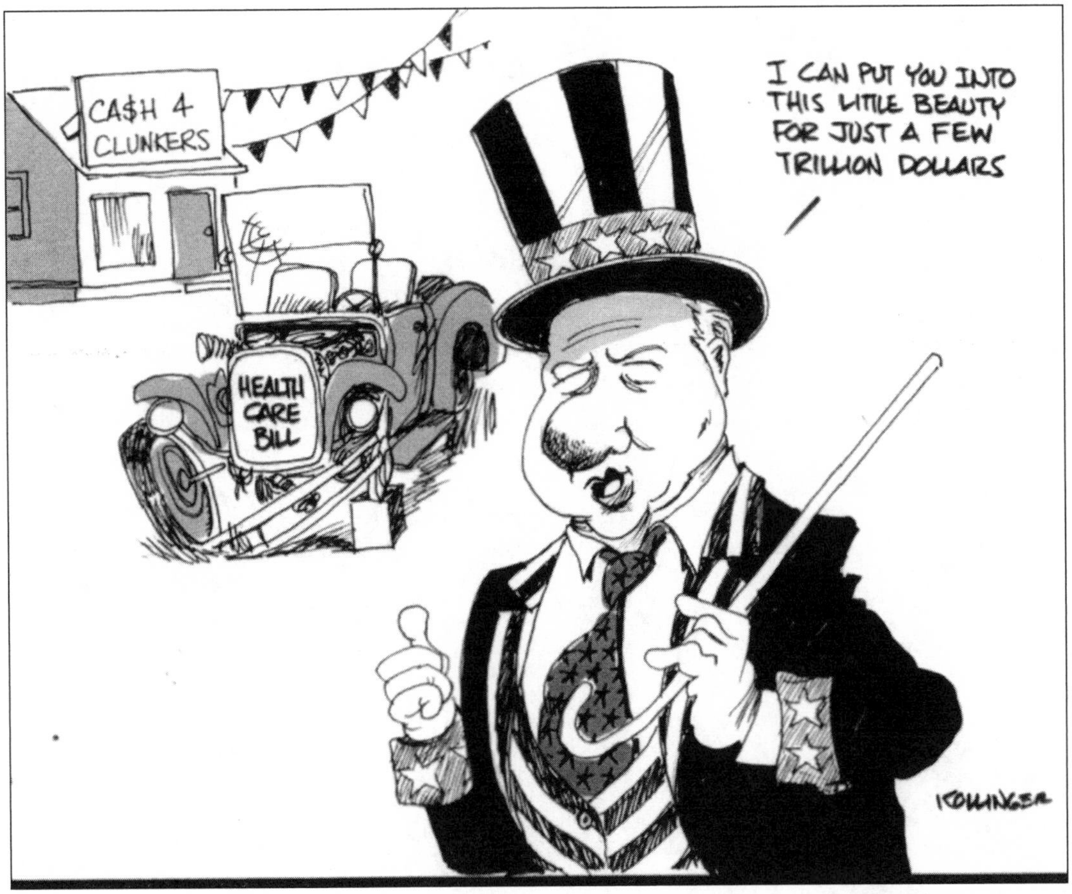
CA$H 4 CLUNKERS
I CAN PUT YOU INTO THIS LITTLE BEAUTY FOR JUST A FEW TRILLION DOLLARS
HEALTH CARE BILL
KOLLINGER

RICK KOLLINGER
Courtesy Star-Democrat (Md.)

HAP PITKIN
Courtesy Boulder Daily Camera

LOOK, EVERYONE KNOWS A GOVERNMENT-RUN, PUBLIC OPTION FOR HEALTH CARE WON'T WORK...
AND BESIDES, WAY TOO MANY PEOPLE WOULD SIGN UP FOR IT.
PITKIN '09
BOULDER CAMERA

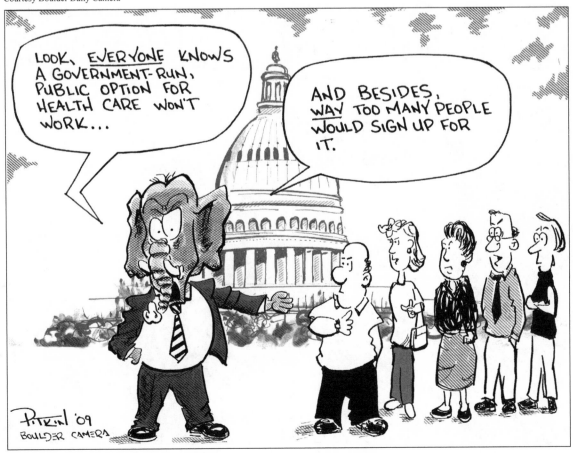

RUN, JOYCE! RUN FOR YOUR LIFE!
GOODNESS, BOBBY! WHAT IS IT?
SOCIALIZED MEDICINE!
ABSORBING EVERYTHING IN ITS PATH!
Gasp!
QUICK! GRAB THE KIDS! AND THE DOG! AND...
OMIGOD! IT'S GOT NANA!
DON'T BE SILLY, ROBERT...
...I'VE HAD MEDICARE FOR YEARS!
AND IS THAT CONGRESSMAN PHILPOCKET?
OH YES, BOB! GREAT COVERAGE, TOO...
...THOUGH I'D FIGHT TO THE DEATH TO KEEP YOU FROM GETTING IT.
THANKS, BUT I FEAR WE ARE DOOMED...
DOOMED!
AND BY "WE" I MEAN OUR PRECIOUS TRANSNATIONAL (choke, sob!) INSURANCE CONGLOMERATES. (blubber, sniff)
AT LEAST THEY'LL BE INSURED, HON.
©2009 Tim Eagan

TIM EAGAN
Courtesy timeagan@cruzio.com

ED GAMBLE
Courtesy Florida Times-Union

We don't need the Government taking over our Health care system!
We agree! so what's your plan?
GOP
GAMBLE ©2009 The FLORIDA TIMES-UNION
We don't need the Government taking over our Health care System!
GOP

DAN FITZGERALD
Courtesy Courier-Journal (Ky.)

WALT HANDELSMAN
Courtesy Newsday

JERRY BARNETT
Courtesy Boonville Standard (Ind.)

WILLIAM FLINT
Courtesy Dallas Morning News

JOSEPH LICCAR
Courtesy Gatehouse Media Examiner

OUTRAGEOUS!!
HEALTH CARE REFORM
TOTAL COST: $1 trillion
UNNECESSARY WAR
TOTAL COST: $3 trillion
ADAM ZYGLIS ©2009 ADAMZYGLIS.COM THEBUFFALONEWS

ADAM ZYGLIS
Courtesy Buffalo News

MARK STREETER
Courtesy Savannah Morning News

The STARS ARE, at LAST, ALIGNED to PASS HEALTH CARE REFORM LEGISLATION THIS YEAR!
PARTISANSHIP
HEY! I GET TO MAKE A WISH!
INSURANCE $ INDUSTRY
SAVANNAHNOW.COM
MSTREETER SAVANNAH MORNING NEWS © 8.28 '09

SUMMERS ©2009 ORLANDO SENTINEL
I'M EVICTING YOU SO I CAN PAY FOR HEALTH CARE... WHAT'S SO FUNNY?...
D.C. Home Sweet Home
FRAUD
WASTE
ABUSE
chips
PIZZA

DANA SUMMERS
Courtesy Orlando Sentinel

LARRY WRIGHT
Courtesy Detroit News

THERE'S PROBABLY ONLY ONE POSSIBLE PROBLEM LEFT FOR HEALTH CARE REFORM...
NEW HEALTH CARE MEDICAL APPOINTMENTS
I'LL PUT YOU ON HOLD!
YOU'RE ON HOLD!
ON HOLD!
YOU'RE ON HOLD!
RING RING RING RING RING
©2009 LARRY WRIGHT THE DETROIT NEWS

2009 © CREATORS.COM
GARY MARKSTEIN
AT LEAST BOTH SIDES HAVE FOUND SOMETHING IN COMMON...
CONSERVATIVES
OBAMA HEALTH REFORM
LIBERALS

GARY MARKSTEIN
Courtesy Creators News Service

J.R. ROSE
Courtesy Byrd Newspapers

NOW!
IT'S NOW OR NEVER FOR NATIONAL HEALTH CARE.
NEVER!
DEMS
GOP
JRROSE! ©2009 BYRD NEWSPAPERS

DOUG MACGREGOR
Courtesy The News-Press (Fla.)

RICHARD BARTHOLOMEW
Courtesy Artizans.com

PETER DUNLAP-SHOHL
Courtesy Anchorage Daily News

I BROUGHT OBAMA'S "DEATH PANELS" TO LIGHT.
NOW IT'S TIME TO GO AFTER THE BOY SCOUTS AND THEIR DIRECTIVE TO DRAG OLD LADIES INTO TRAFFIC!
FRONTIERSMAN 2009

CHUCK LEGGE
Courtesy The Frontiersman

NICK ANDERSON
Courtesy Houston Chronicle

HEALTH CARE
REFORM
LIES
MYTHS
NICK ANDERSON
©9.13.09
HOUSTON CHRONICLE

YOU'RE FINE. TAKE TWO ASPIRINS. IT'S ALL IN YOUR HEAD...
EEEEEEEEEEEEEEEEEEEEEEEE
PING!
DR. STATUS QUO
U.S. HEALTH SYSTEM
CAGLECARTOONS.COM
JEFF PARKER ©2009 FLORIDA TODAY

JEFF PARKER
Courtesy Florida Today

DICK LOCHER
Courtesy Chicago Tribune

SO WE'RE CROSSING INTO THE UNITED STATES. WHO'S GOING TO STOP US?
SWINE FLU
MEXICO
©2009 CHICAGO TRIBUNE

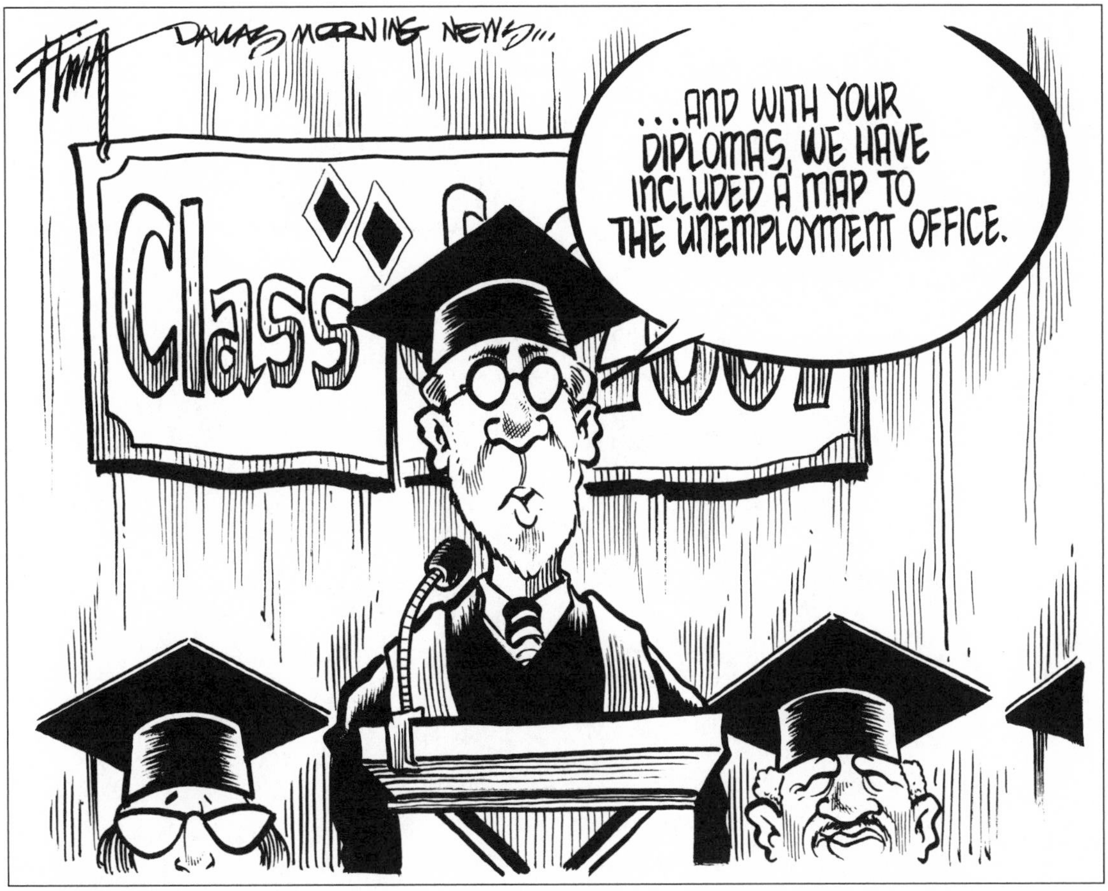
DALLAS MORNING NEWS
...AND WITH YOUR DIPLOMAS, WE HAVE INCLUDED A MAP TO THE UNEMPLOYMENT OFFICE.
Class

WILLIAM FLINT
Courtesy Dallas Morning News

DENNIS DRAUGHON
Courtesy The Insider (N.C.)

DRAUGHON THE INSIDER
SIGH...
TINK
SCHOOL
WELCOME BACK TO INCREASED CLASS SIZES & SCHOOL BUDGET CUTS
SIGH...

SAGE STOSSEL
Courtesy Atlantic Monthly

JIM DYKE
Courtesy Jefferson City
News Tribune (Mo.)

MARC MURPHY
Courtesy The Courier-Journal (Ky.)

WOW. A MOTHER'S DAY CARD AND A CHECK YOU WROTE ME FOR 75 BILLION DOLLARS.
WE'RE LEARNING A LOT FROM PRESIDENT OBAMA AT SCHOOL.
©2009 LARRY WRIGHT
THE DETROIT NEWS

LARRY WRIGHT
Courtesy Detroit News

KIRK ANDERSON
Courtesy Artizans Entertainment

KIRK ©'09
WWW.KIRKTOONS.COM
HMO

NO! KIDS!! DON'T LISSEN TO HIM!
HE'S TRYIN' TO INDOCTRINIZATE YOUR BRAINS!
COVER YOUR EARS!
NOTZEE
HE'S A SOSHLIST!
I ♥ PALIN
RUN!
DON'T LOOK INTO HIS EYES!!
SCHOOLS SPEECH
...AND THIS IS WHY IT'S SO IMPORTANT TO GET A GOOD EDUCATION.
CAGLECARTOONS.COM
JOHN COLE
©THE TIMES-TRIBUNE
SCRANTON, PA

JOHN COLE
Courtesy Scranton Times-Tribune

PHIL HANDS
Courtesy Wisconsin State Journal

IF TEACHERS GRADED THE SAME WAY THEY WERE PAID...
EXAM RESULTS
IT DOESN'T MATTER HOW HARD YOU WORKED OR HOW WELL YOU PERFORMED, EVERYBODY GETS THE SAME GRADE.
EXCEPT FOR TIMMY WHO HAS THE MOST SENIORITY BECAUSE HE'S BEEN IN THE SECOND GRADE THE LONGEST.
A
B
PHIL HANDS
WISCONSIN STATE JOURNAL 2009

Town Hall Meetings

Citizens across the country in 2009 took part in town hall meetings to express their views on health care and other issues to their representatives. The meetings were sometimes raucous, as opponents to government-run health care vociferously made their opinions known. Many legislators faced forceful questioning from their constituents. Polls showed a majority of Americans opposed President Obama's health care reform plan. Some legislators, fearing hostile crowds, opted not to attend town hall meetings.

This grass-roots movement also found voice in "tea party" tax protests and a march on Washington that attracted tens of thousands of demonstrators. The crowds were dismissed by many Democrats as "astro-turf" and "unruly mobs."

Columnists and Washington pundits reported they had never seen such a spontaneous movement by average citizens, many of whom were taking part in the national dialogue for the first time. Protesters responded to observers from Canada and Great Britain, who warned the U.S. not to go down the same road they had traveled to socialized medicine, with its long waiting lines and reduced care for the elderly.

MIKE PETERS
Courtesy Dayton Daily News

SPORTS
DURING THE HOCKEY GAME LAST NIGHT A TOWN HALL MEETING BROKE OUT
MIKE PETERS
©2009 DAYTON DAILY NEWS KING FEATURES SYN

I LIKED IT BETTER WHEN THEY WORE THOSE LITTLE TINFOIL HATS TO PREVENT MIND CONTROL!
GLENN BECK ... GLENN BECK ... GLENN
FOX NEWS ... FOX NEWS ... FOX N
RUSH LIMBAUGH ... RUSH LIM
MUST... GO... TO... HEALTH... CARE... TOWN... MEETING... RAISE... RUCKUS...
©2009 MIKE MARLAND CONCORD MONITOR
marlandcartoons.com

MIKE MARLAND
Courtesy Concord Monitor

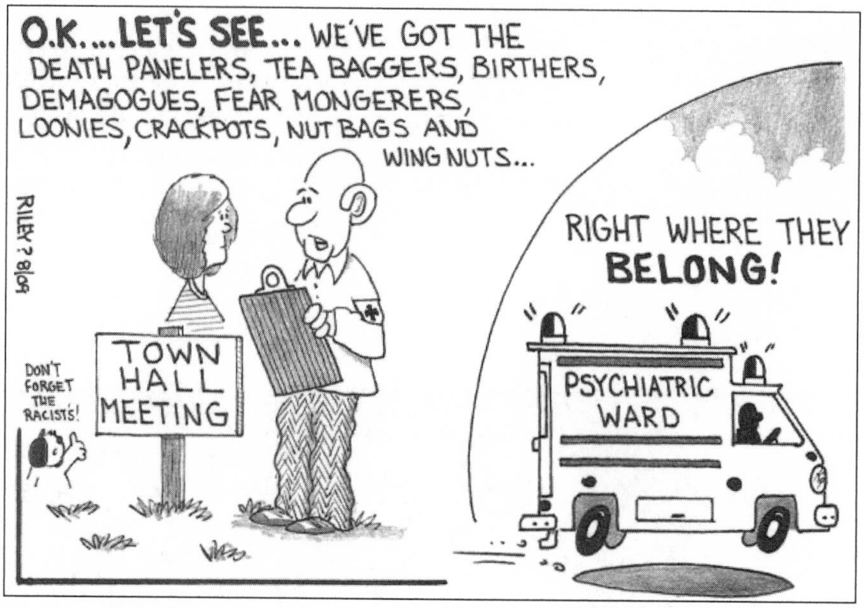
O.K.... LET'S SEE... WE'VE GOT THE DEATH PANELERS, TEA BAGGERS, BIRTHERS, DEMAGOGUES, FEAR MONGERERS, LOONIES, CRACKPOTS, NUT BAGS AND WING NUTS...
RIGHT WHERE THEY BELONG!
TOWN HALL MEETING
DON'T FORGET THE RACISTS!
PSYCHIATRIC WARD
RILEY 8/09

JOHN RILEY
Courtesy johnrileycartoons.com

DANA SUMMERS
Courtesy Orlando Sentinel

TOWN HALL
©2009 SUMMERS ORLANDO SENTINEL
I'M YOUR CONGRESSMAN AND I'M HERE TO DISCUSS HEALTH CARE.

What I didn't do on my Summer Vacation:
1) I didn't shout at or shove anybody.
2) I didn't bully anybody or bite anyone's finger off.
3) I didn't use my outside voice inside.
4) I didn't call anybody ugly or hurtful names.
5) I didn't refuse to play well with others.
6) I didn't throw any temper tantrums.
7) I didn't tell stories or make up things that weren't true.
In other words, I didn't attend any Town Hall meetings with any so-called grownups!
A GOOD SUMMER.
SAVANNAHNOW.COM
MSTREETER
SAVANNAH MORNING NEWS 9.4 09

MARK STREETER
Courtesy Savannah Morning News

DAVID HITCH
Courtesy Worcester Telegram & Gazette (Mass.)

WE'RE MAD AS
SAVE OUR WALLETS
ENOUGH IS ENOUGH
THESE TEA PARTY PEOPLE ARE SMOKING MAD! WHAT SHOULD WE DO?!
TAX THEIR CIGARETTES?
HITCH SUNDAY TELEGRAM

THE END IS NEAR!
WHAT'S HAPPENED TO AMERICA??
NATIONAL HYSTERIA PARTY HEADQUARTERS
HOPE HYSTERIA ISN'T CONTAGIOUS.
WATCH OUT FOR THE PRESIDENT! HE'S DANGEROUS!
KEEP HIM AWAY FROM THE SCHOOL CHILDREN!!
SIGNS
THEY'RE FASCISTS
SOCIALISTS
DANGEROUS
FOREIGN
© Cleaves'09

ANN CLEAVES
Courtesy Ann Cleaves

JOHN FULLER
Courtesy Artizans.com

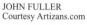

FULLER © 2009
ARTIZANS.COM
THAT NONSENSE? JUST A BUNCH OF WHINING, RIGHT-WING EXTREMIST TAXPAYERS WHO DON'T WANT TO DO THEIR PATRIOTIC DUTY. DON'T WORRY, NOTHING WILL COME OF IT....
TEA

HE'S EXACTLY LIKE HITLER!
IT'S SO TRUE.
HE WANT S DEATH CAMPS FOR GRANNY!!
HEIL BARACK!
ADOLF OBAMA HAS A FINAL SOLUTION FOR DEMOCRACY! I WANT MY COUNTRY BACK!
GOD BLESS AMERIKA
IF ANY NAZIS SHOW UP, WE'S READY FER 'EM!!
TOWN HALL SHOUTING MATCHES
ROCKET LAUNCHER
X 5000
BRING IT ON, MUSSOLINI!
AMMO
AMMO
AMMO
OPEN-CARRY AIN'T SO SCARY
WHY DON'T YOU TAKE US MORE SERIOUSLY?
OBAMA
©CAGLECARTOONS.COM 09

CHRIS BRITT
Courtesy State Journal-Register (Ill.)

JESSE SPRINGER
Courtesy Eugene Register-Guard

SPRINGER ©2009
www.springercreative.com
AT A TOWN HALL MEETING NEAR YOU...
Healthcare for all sounds good, but I am concerned about how that will affect me and my family...
THIS IS YOUR BRAIN.
OBAMACARE will REQUIRE MANDATORY NOSTRIL ENLARGEMENT SURGERY for all Left-Handed BABIES!!!
THIS IS YOUR BRAIN ON RIGHT-WING TALK RADIO. ANY QUESTIONS?

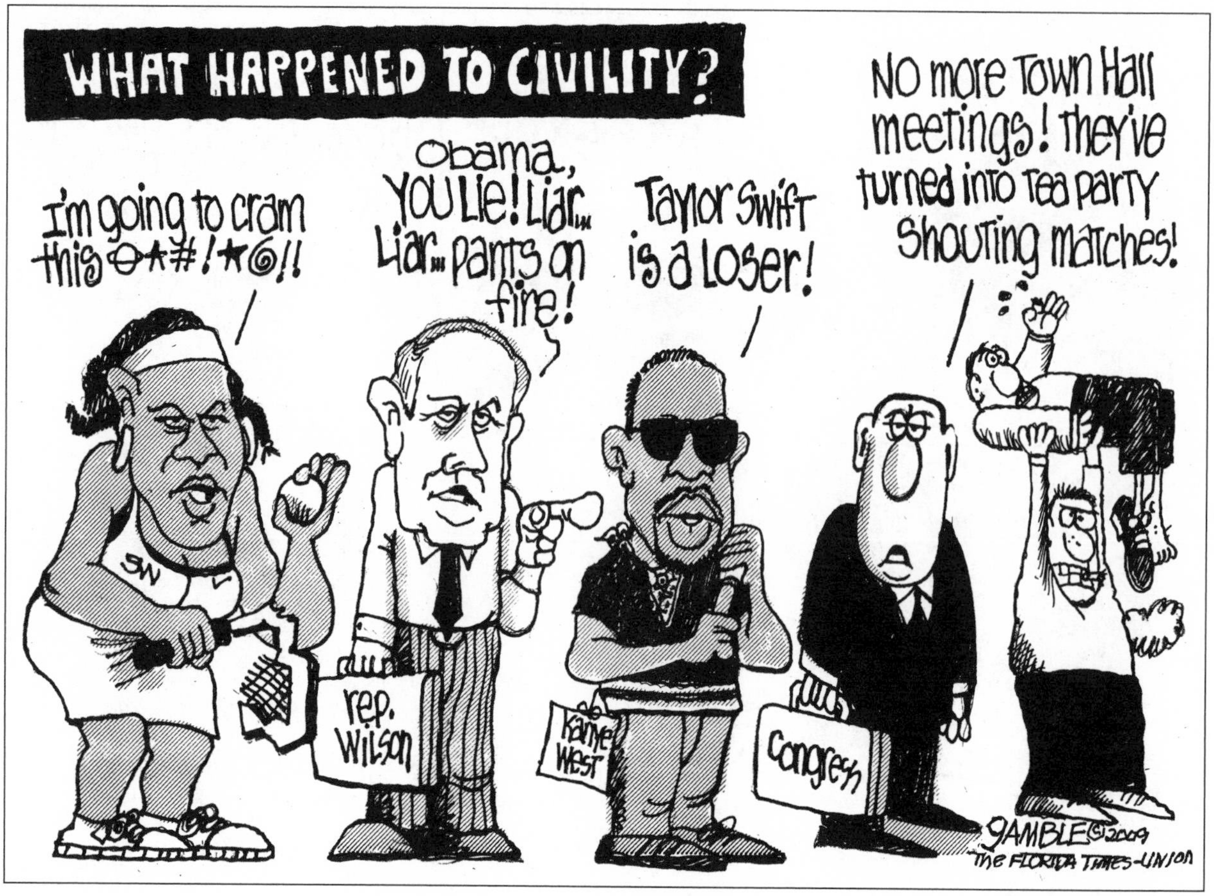

WHAT HAPPENED TO CIVILITY?
I'm going to cram this @*#!★@!!
Obama, YOU LIE! Liar... Liar... pants on fire!
Taylor Swift is a Loser!
No more Town Hall meetings! They've turned into Tea party shouting matches!
SW
rep. Wilson
Kanye West
Congress
GAMBLE© 2009 The FLORIDA TIMES-UNION

ED GAMBLE
Courtesy Florida Times-Union

NATE BEELER
Courtesy Washington Examiner

BEELER ©09 The Washington Examiner CAGLECARTOONS.COM
I WILL NO ANY BILL ONE DIM
YO! SORRY TO INTERRUPT YER $#☆!☠ CARTOON, BUT I WANNA GIVE SHOUT OUTS TO MY BOYS REP. JOE WILSON AND KANYE!!!
HEAL
ANS HANGE IEVE IN.
INCIVILITY

Society

Public civility seems to be on the wane. Rep. Joe Wilson shouted "You lie" during a speech by President Obama to a joint session of Congress. During the 2009 MTV Video Music Awards, while Taylor Swift was accepting her award for Best Female Video, singer Kanye West disrupted the show. He dashed on stage and proclaimed that Beyonce's video for "Single Ladies," nominated for the same award, was "one of the best videos of all time."

Gun sales spiked prior to Obama's inauguration, as many feared a liberal push could threaten gun ownership rights. A poll showed that children play outside an average of only a few minutes a day, leading to obesity and other health problems. Besides health worries, future generations face a massive U.S. debt. Many fear nationalized health care will lead to long waiting times for treatment.

U.S. manufacturing continued its slump, with China poised to dominate future world markets. Michael Jackson's death held the public's attention more than far weightier issues. More and more of American everyday life seems to be tied to government — local, state, and federal. The use of cell phones by automobile drivers has made America's highways much more dangerous.

CHRIS BRITT
Courtesy State Journal-Register (Ill.)

HEALTH-CARE REFORM IS BEING DISCUSSED.
THE ECONOMY IS STILL IN THE TANK.
U.S. TROOPS CONTINUE TO DIE IN IRAQ AND AFGHANISTAN.
BRITT
7-8
©09
AND NOW... MORE ON MICHAEL JACKSON.

DO THESE STRESS BALLS COME ANY LARGER?
STAHLER 1/3
© 2009 Jeff Stahler/ Dist. by NEA, Inc.
www.comics.com

JEFF STAHLER
Courtesy NEA

Your choice, driver... Booze or cell? Same results!
VODKA
EVANS ©09

PETER EVANS
Courtesy Islander News (Fla.)

DOUG REGALIA
Courtesy Contra Costa Times (Calif.)

HOW OUR KIDS RECEIVE CONFLICTING MESSAGES
JUST SAY NO TO DRUGS
IN A SERIES
DOUG@MRCPA.COM

PHIL HANDS
Courtesy Wisconsin State Journal

JON RICHARDS
Courtesy Albuquerque Journal North

The Secretary of the Interior noted that American children spend a daily average of only four minutes outside.
Outside what?
©2009 Stephanie McMillan

STEPHANIE MCMILLAN
Courtesy Los Angeles Times

© Tim Jackson 2009 090402
DTV
OKAY— A BIT TO THE LEFT. HIGHER---HIGHER--- NO . . . DOWN SOME. A SKOSH MORE--- GOT IT! PERFECT! NOW DON'T MOVE!!!
DIGITAL REVOLUTION, HAH! THAT'S THE SAME THING WE HAD'a DO BACK IN THE '60s
HDTV ANTENNA
obita@clstoons.com

TIM JACKSON
Courtesy Chicago Defender

JOE HELLER
Courtesy Green Bay Press & Gazette

TWITTER- CONSTANTLY UPDATING YOUR FRIENDS
JITTER- CONSTANTLY CHECKING YOUR 401(k)
FRITTER- CONSTANTLY WORRYING ABOUT YOUR JOB & HOME
BITTER- CONSTANTLY HEARING ABOUT BIG FINANCIAL BAILOUTS
AIG $
JoeHeller ©2009 GREEN BAY PRESS GAZ.

IF YOU EVER CHEAT ON ME, I WON'T BE AT THE PRESS CONFERENCE.
BUT WE'RE NOT FAMOUS...
WHY WOULD THERE BE A PRESS CONFERENCE?
BECAUSE OF THE HOMICIDE.
THE TIMES-PICAYUNE © 2009
S.KELLEY

STEVE KELLEY
Courtesy The Times Picayune (La.)

TIM EAGAN
Courtesy timeagan@cruzio.com

IT'S 2075, AND EARTH IS DYING...
THEN, HOPE!...
ASTRO-EXPLORERS DISCOVER A TWIN EARTH! AN EDEN!
PLUS, WE COULD HAVE IT ALL TO OURSELVES!
IF ONLY WE COULD GET THERE.
FEAR NOT!...
WE HAVE A PLAN!
BUT IT WILL TAKE YOUR TOTAL COOPERATION!
AND ALL OF YOUR MONEY!
MAIL@TIMEAGAN.COM
OF COURSE, THERE'S NO WAY THAT'S GONNA HAPPEN!
TYPICAL!
ANOTHER BIG GOVERNMENT PROGRAM!
BUT WE'RE ALL GOING TO DIE.
ARE WE? DID YOU EVEN CONSIDER TAX CUTS FOR PRAYING?
©2009

THERE ARE MORE GUNS THAN PEOPLE IN AMERICA
I KNOW... IT'S INSANE!
BLAT-A-TAT TATTA-TAT A-TAT-A-ATTA-TAT BLAT-AT-TAT-TAT-TAT
AND THE RATIO GROWS!
JOEL PETT
3/13/9 LEXINGTON HERALD-LEADER

JOEL PETT
Courtesy Lexington Herald-Leader

I THINK THIS IS WHAT THEY CALL A "TIPPING POINT."
C.Beyl
© 2-15-09

CHARLES BEYL
Courtesy Lancaster Sunday News (Pa.)

PETER DUNLAP-SHOHL
Courtesy Anchorage Daily News

AN EYE, FOR AN EYE, A LIFE FOR A LIFE.
...SO WHEN WE FIND THE STATE HAS FRIED SOMEONE INNOCENT, DO WE HOLD A LOTTERY, OR MAY I JUST COME FOR YOU?
DUNLAP-SHOHL ©2009

SO LET THIS ALL BE A LESSON TO YOU, SON—
WORK HARD, FOLLOW THE RULES, LIVE WITHIN YOUR MEANS AND ONE DAY YOU TOO CAN BAIL OUT THOSE WHO DIDN'T....
©2009
Auchter
GRAND RAPIDS BUSINESS JOURNAL
auchtoon.com

JOHN AUCHTER
Courtesy Grand Rapids Business Journal

WAYNE STROOT
Courtesy Hastings Tribune (Neb.)

©'09 THE STROOT HASTINGS TRIBUNE
GET A JOB.
MEDICARE/ SOC. SECURITY GOING BROKE SOONER

DAD-
WHAT'S
LABOR
DAY?
IT'S A DAY SET ASIDE TO
HONOR ALL THE PEOPLE THAT
WORK TO MAKE THE THINGS
THAT WE NEED!
YOU MEAN
THE
CHINESE?

BRUCE QUAST
Courtesy Rockford Register-Star (Ill.)

Sweating Bullets
THAT NUT
OBAMA AND
THE DEMOCRATS
ARE GONNA
TAKE OUR
GUNS AWAY!
GUN SALES
SMOKING SINCE
OBAMA'S WIN
CAGLECARTOONS.COM

JEFF PARKER
Courtesy Florida Today

JOE HELLER
Courtesy Green Bay Press & Gazette

PUBLIC-OPTION HEALTH CARE?
THAT SMACKS OF
SOCIALISM!*
* AS THEY LISTEN TO TALK RADIO ON GOV'T REGULATED AIRWAVES...
IN A VEHICLE FROM A GOV'T BAILED-OUT COMPANY...
DRIVING ON A GOV'T BUILT INTERSTATE HIGHWAY...
THIS PUBLICLY-EDUCATED FAMILY...
IS SIPPING WATER FROM A MUNICIPAL SYSTEM...
ON IT'S WAY TO VACATION AT A NATIONAL PARK.

OH MY GOODNESS! WHAT HAPPENED TO YOU? DID YOU GET MUGGED??
WE GOT INTO A HEALTH CARE DISCUSSION AT THE OFFICE...
danielc@knoxnews.com
DANIEL ©NEWS SENTINEL

CHARLIE DANIEL
Courtesy Knoxville News-Sentinel

IN MY COUNTRY, I'M ALL FOR THE MARRIAGE OF BLEACH AND SILICONE
CALIFORNIA
KRANKY ©'09
www.krankyscartoons.com

JOSEPH RANK
Courtesy Times-Press-Recorder (Calif.)

JOHN AUCHTER
Courtesy Grand Rapids Business Journal

GOVERNMENT!
Where do children learn such filthy language?
Tonight on FoxNews...
©2009 Auchter GRAND RAPIDS BUSINESS JOURNAL
auchtoon.com

SUMMER 2009
HONEY... MY BATTERY IS DEAD. COULD YOU TWEET SISSY TO PASS THE KETCHUP... HONEY?
C.Beyl
©8-2-09 SUNDAY NEWS, LANCASTER, PA

CHARLES BEYL
Courtesy Lancaster Sunday News (Pa.)

ELIZABETH BRICQUET
Courtesy Kingsport Times-News (Tenn.)

WE KNEW SHE WAS ONE OF US WHEN WE REALIZED HER BROKEN WRIST WAS AN OLD 'TEXTING' INJURY..
IDA
TAP TAP TAP TEXT
TAP TAP
TAP TAP TAP TEXT

Politics

Longtime Republican Sen. Arlen Specter of Pennsylvania, trailing badly in early election polls, switched to the Democratic Party. Illinois Gov. Rod Blagojevich was accused of trying to sell the U.S. Senate seat formerly held by Barack Obama and was forced out of office. Blagojevich eventually appointed Roland Burris to the post. Calls for Burris' resignation began after allegations surfaced that he had not been candid about his contacts with associates of Blagojevich.

Gov. Mark Sanford of South Carolina disappeared for several days in June after telling his staff he would be hiking alone on the Appalachian Trail. Upon his return the married governor announced that he had flown to Argentina to visit a girl friend. Sanford eventually reimbursed taxpayers for some of his travel expenses amid calls for his impeachment.

Sarah Palin resigned as governor of Alaska, reportedly signed a multi-million-dollar book deal, and launched a public speaking career. She gave every indication of considering a run for the presidency.

Blue Dog Democrats, representing conservative areas of the country, tended to vote with Republicans against Obama's liberal agenda.

JEFF PARKER
Courtesy Florida Today

SOOO... WE ALL MAY BE DENIED REASONABLE HEALTHCARE REFORM BECAUSE OF THEIR PRE-EXISTING CONDITION -- ACUTE PARTISANITIS.
JEFF PARKER
©2009 FLORIDA TODAY
CAGLECARTOONS.COM

WHO'S GONNA SKIN IT?
I QUIT!
Palin
VIC HARVILLE

VIC HARVILLE
Courtesy Stephens Media

JOE HELLER
Courtesy Green Bay Press & Gazette

The First 100 Days...
That's like 700 in Dog Days...
or 8 years in Republican Days.
OBAMA'S AGENDA
BO
UNDOING THE BUSH YEARS
JOE HELLER

ED HALL
Courtesy Baker County Press (Fla.)

TODAY'S WORD OF THE DAY:
"Presidency"
• n. 1 The process whereby a fairly normal human being is transformed into a hook...
upon which are hung all of the hopes and dreams of one group of people,...
and all of the fears and hatreds of another.
PITKIN '09
BOULDER CAMERA

HAP PITKIN
Courtesy Boulder Daily Camera

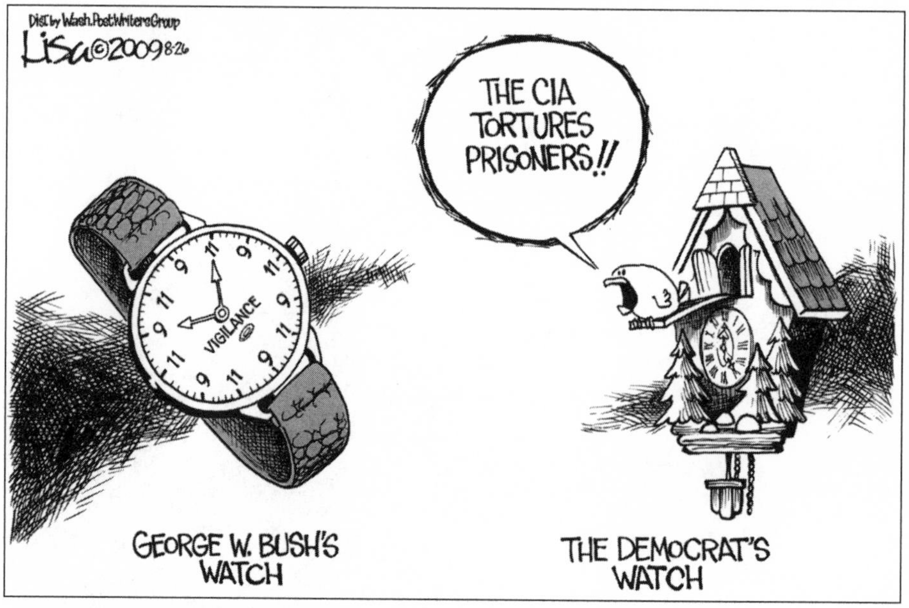
Dist by Wash.PostWritersGroup
Lisa ©2009 8-26
THE CIA TORTURES PRISONERS!!
VIGILANCE
GEORGE W. BUSH'S WATCH
THE DEMOCRAT'S WATCH

LISA BENSON
Courtesy Washington Post Writers Group

DICK LOCHER
Courtesy Chicago Tribune

I GET THE FEELING I'M NOT IN THE MAINSTREAM ANYMORE.
GOP

YOU AIN'T NOTHIN' BUT A BLUE DOG..
GROWLIN' ALL THE TIME!
YOU AIN'T NEVER VOTED MY WAY
AND YOU AIN'T NO FRIEND OF MINE!
OBAMA
GRRRRR
NATIONAL NEWS
CONSERVATIVE DEMOCRATS STALL OBAMA-CARE
'09
RICKY NOBILE

RICKY NOBILE
Courtesy Ricky Nobile Cartoons

ROBERT ARIAIL
Courtesy robertariail.com

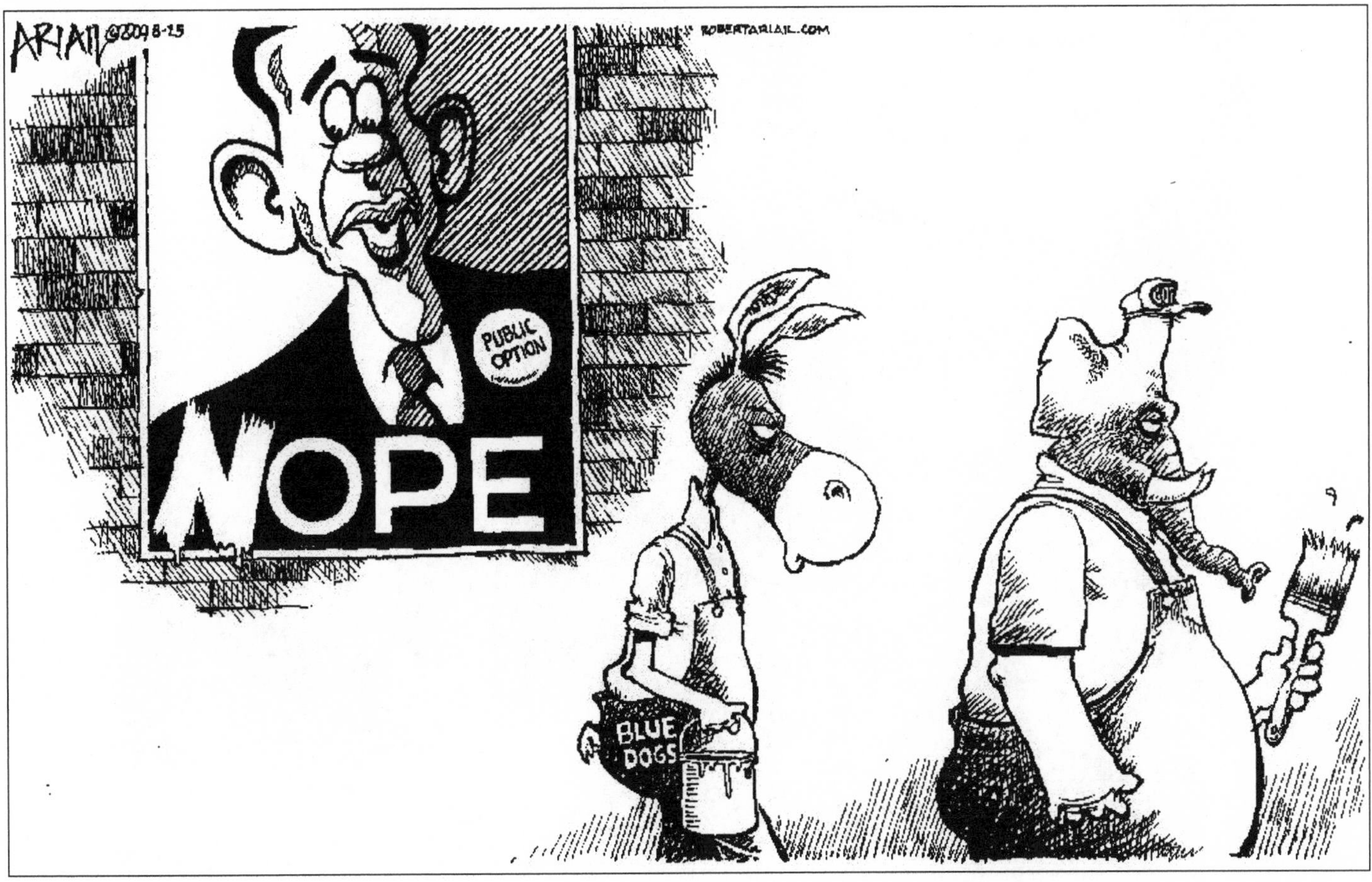
ARIAIL ©2009 8-25
ROBERTARIAIL.COM
PUBLIC OPTION
NOPE
BLUE DOGS

ALL U.S. PRESIDENTS GATHER FOR A WHITE HOUSE LUNCHEON TO GIVE OBAMA ADVICE...
KEEP THE COUNTRY SAFE.
DON'T RAISE TAXES.
TAKE CARE OF THE POOR.
STAY AWAY FROM INTERNS.
©2009 JRROSE! BYRD NEWSPAPERS OF VA.

J.R. ROSE
Courtesy Byrd Newspapers

WILLIAM WARREN
Courtesy Americans For Limited Government

FOR AMERICANS FOR LIMITED GOVERNMENT ©2009 WILLIAM WARREN
THOSE PESKY BLUE DOGS ARE NOT COOPERATING ON HEALTHCARE!
DON'T WORRY. I'VE MADE ARRANGEMENTS...
SOMEONE CALLED?
VICK
VICK
7

CLAY BENNETT
Courtesy Chattanooga Times-Free Press

JOHN TREVER
Courtesy Albuquerque Journal

SHE'S NOT SO DUMB AFTER ALL!
I THOUGHT I WON!
MULTI-MILLION DOLLAR BOOK DEAL
SARAH PALIN
BIDEN
VICE PRESIDENT
RICKY NOBILE '09

RICKY NOBILE
Courtesy Ricky Nobile Cartoons

WHY DOING THAT?!
I HAVE NO IDEA!
NO PARACHUTE AT ALL!
ALASKA GOVERNORSHIP
SARAH PALIN
SUICIDAL ACT
POL© GALVEZ

POL GALVEZ
Courtesy Philippine News

CHUCK LEGGE
Courtesy The Frontiersman

I'M STEPPING DOWN

BRUCE MACKINNON
Courtesy Halifax Herald (Can.)

2009 © FULLER
ARTIZANS.COM
HI, I'M HILLARY CLINTON. PEOPLE USED TO FEAR ME!....
GIT YER OWN SIP SACK.

A DAY IN THE LIFE OF THE SECRETARY OF STATE

JOHN FULLER
Courtesy Artizans.com

JOHN SHERFFIUS
Courtesy Boulder Camera

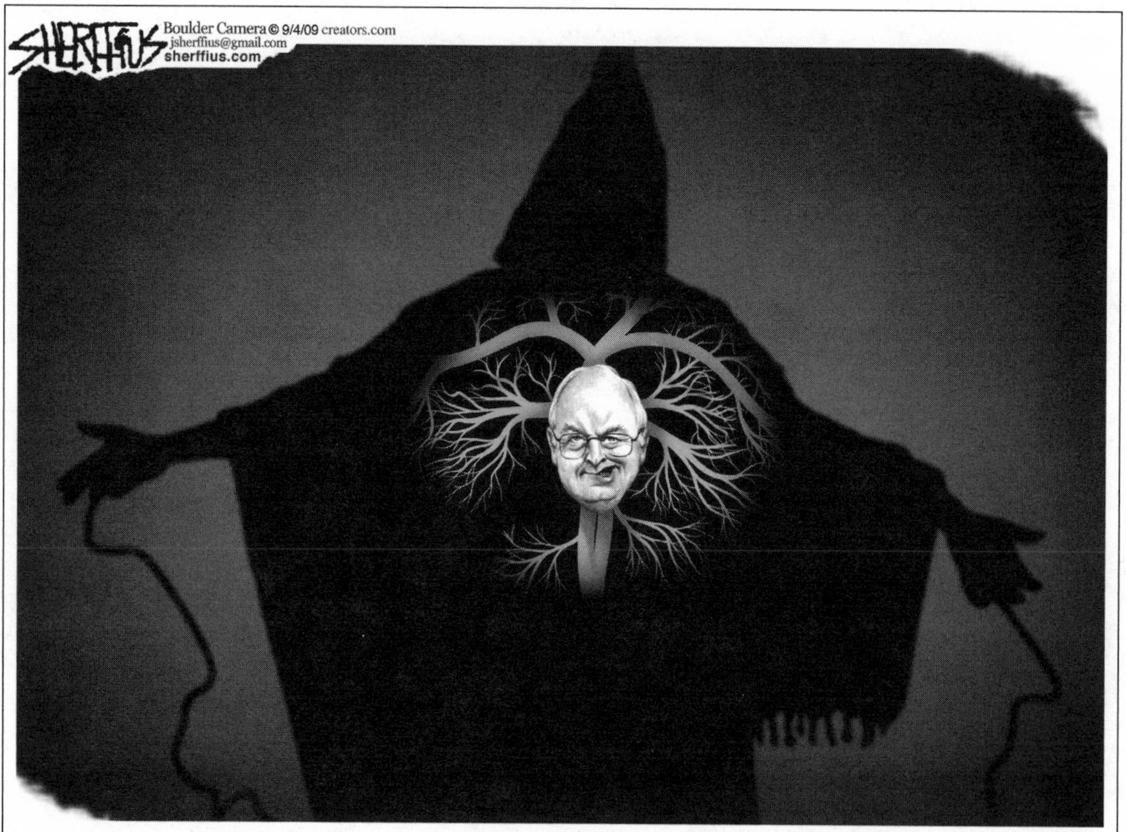
SHERFFIUS
Boulder Camera © 9/4/09 creators.com
jsherffius@gmail.com
sherffius.com

The heart of darkness

REMEMBER THE REPUBLICANS' BRIDGE TO NOWHERE?
VOTERS
OINK!
OINK!
NOW IT'S...
WHAT ARE THE DEMOCRATS BUILDING?
THE ROAD TO SERFDOM!
3 '09 CHUCK ASAY
©2009 CREATORS SYNDICATE, INC www.creators.com

CHUCK ASAY
Courtesy Creators Syndicate

ROBERT ARIAIL
Courtesy robertariail.com

OUR PLAN IS TO WAIT THEM OUT UNTIL THEIR SYSTEM IMPLODES AND THEY CHANGE TO OUR FORM OF GOVERNMENT ...
GOP
CUBA POLICY
ARIAIL ©2009 4-8
OUR PLAN, TOO - AND IT SEEMS TO HAVE WORKED.
CUBA
DEMS
OBAMA'S SOCIALIST AGENDA
BANKS, CAR COS., HEALTH CARE AND ENTITLEMENTS

CORREO AEREO
Governor Mark Sanford
Governor's Mansion
Columbia SC
USA
Don't cry for me
Argentina

GUY BADEAUX
Courtesy Le Droit (Canada)

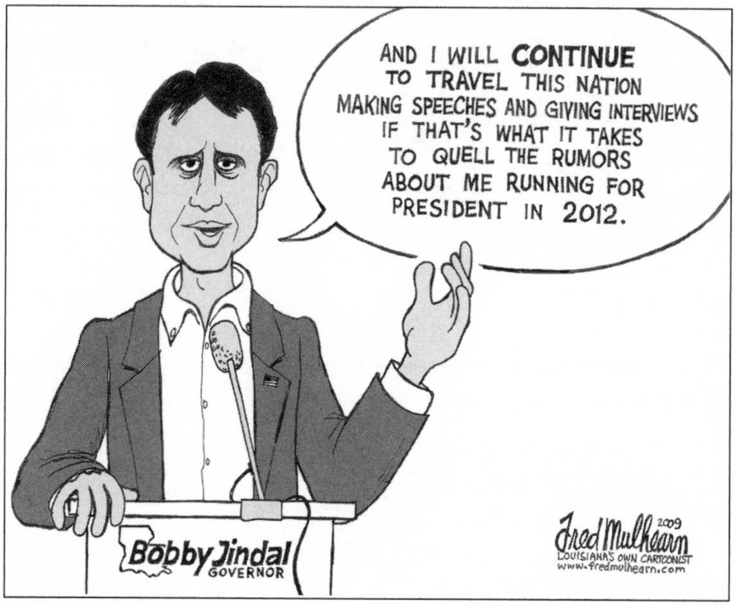
AND I WILL CONTINUE TO TRAVEL THIS NATION MAKING SPEECHES AND GIVING INTERVIEWS IF THAT'S WHAT IT TAKES TO QUELL THE RUMORS ABOUT ME RUNNING FOR PRESIDENT IN 2012.
Bobby Jindal
GOVERNOR
Fred Mulhearn 2009
LOUISIANA'S OWN CARTOONIST
www.fredmulhearn.com

FRED MULHEARN
Courtesy fredmulhearn.com

GARY VARVEL
Courtesy Indianapolis Star

THEN I SAID, YOU'RE MY SOUL MATE AND SHE WAS LIKE, OMG! AND I WAS LIKE, LOL...
garyvarvel.com
Gov. Sanford won't QUIT

'Moe
Toronto Star
WHO MENTIONED THAT MAN'S NAME?
JEEZ, ALL I SAID WAS HEALTH CARE BILL...

THEO MOUDAKIS
Courtesy Toronto Star

JON RICHARDS
Courtesy Albuquerque Journal North

OH SPIRIT... YOU ARE THE MOST TERRIBLE SHADE OF ALL...
DON'T WORRY, SCROOGE. I'M JUST A RECURRING NIGHTMARE.
POLITICS
ETHICS REFORM
JON RICHARDS

I AM NO LONGER GOVERNOR OF ALASKA ...
I AM MOTHER OF DISASTER!
PALIN FOR ANYTHING THAT GETS ATTENTION
BOILEAU THESTATEJOURNAL 2009

LINDA BOILEAU
Courtesy Frankfort State Journal (Ky.)

©2009 Dayton Daily News King Features Synd.
grimmy.com
Mike Peters
NO
YES WE CAN

MIKE PETERS
Courtesy Dayton Daily News

ED HALL
Courtesy Baker County Press (Fla.)

TOO MESSY...
©2009 ARTIZANS .com

MARK SANFORD SAGA REVEALS:
THE TROUBLE WITH BEING A BIG SHOT IN SOUTH CAROLINA...
ARGENTINE WOMEN WON'T LEAVE YOU ALONE
IT'S A CURSE
PRESS-REGISTER
CROWETOONS.com

J.D. CROWE
Courtesy Mobile Press-Register

MIKE KEEFE
Courtesy Denver Post

Mike Keefe THE DENVER POST 9.12.09
TAPPITY TAP TAP
Dear Joe Wilson,
For attracting all that press attention and for demonstrating that you are the biggest buffoon in South Carolina politics, I have one thing to say:
Many thanks!
Governor Sanford

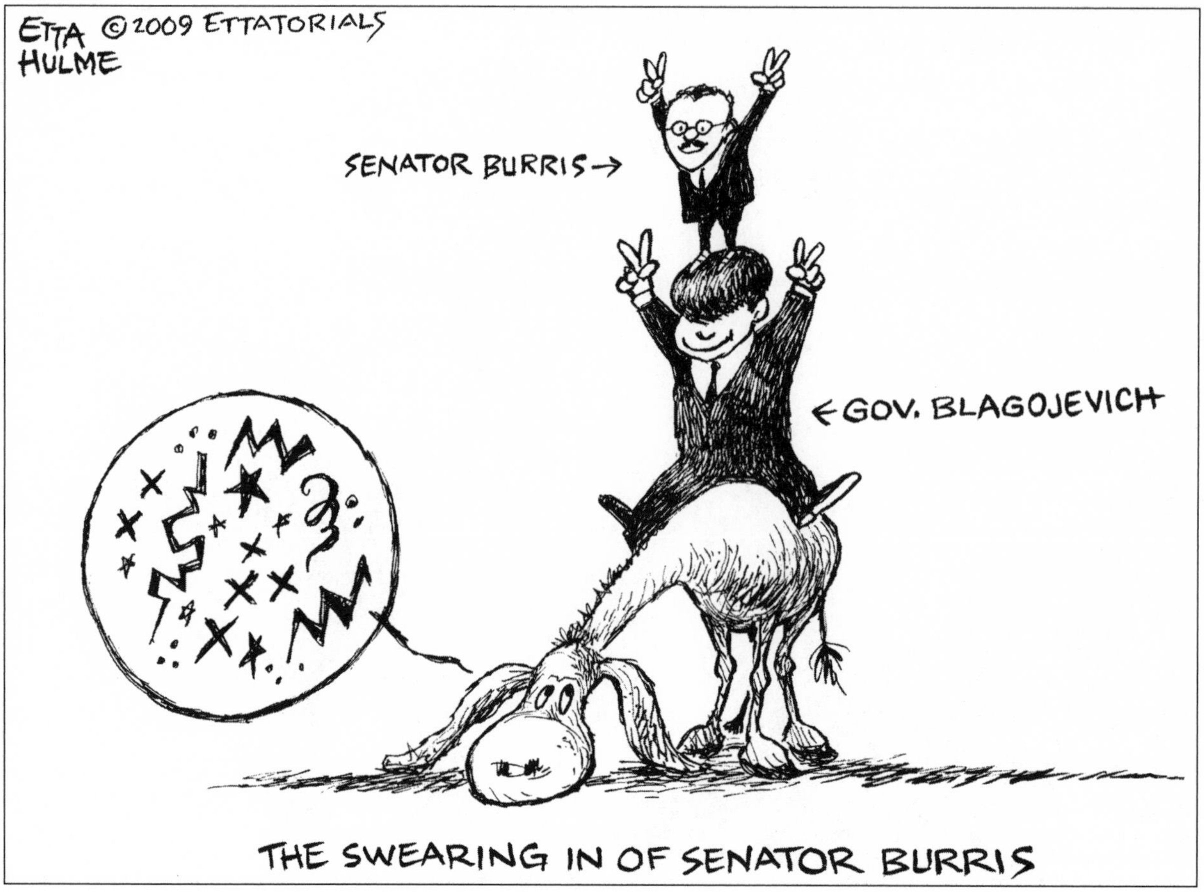

ETTA HULME
Courtesy Fort Worth Star-Telegram

DICK LOCHER
Courtesy Chicago Tribune

I DUNNO -- IT DOESN'T FIT QUITE RIGHT...
EXCELLENT CHOICE, SENATOR! DON'T WORRY -- WE CAN TAKE IN A LITTLE HERE, LET OUT A LITTLE THERE...
JON RICHARDS 4/28/09

JON RICHARDS
Courtesy Albuquerque Journal North

TERRY WISE
Courtesy ratland.com

YOU THINK RONALD REAGAN WOULD APPROVE OF ANYTHING WE'VE DONE THE LAST FEW YEARS ?
I DON'T KNOW... BUT I KEEP HAVING THIS NIGHTMARE WITH HIM STANDING AT THE FOOT OF MY BED WEARING A HOCKEY MASK AND HOLDING A MACHETE.
Terry C Wise 1/09 RATLAND.COM

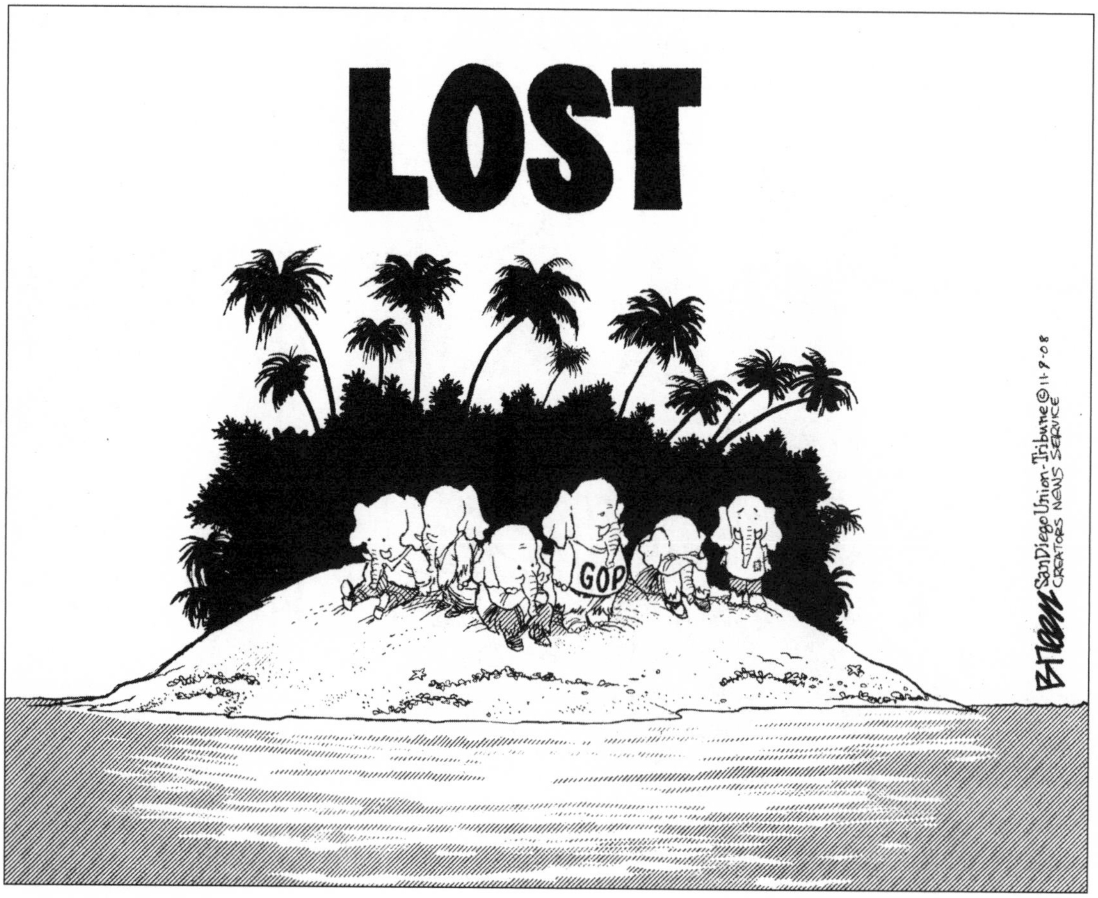

STEVE BREEN
Courtesy San Diego Union-Tribune

ED GAMBLE
Courtesy Florida Times-Union

The Economy

One of the worst economic downturns in U.S. history opened 2009. The gap between what the economy was producing and normal performance was about 10 percent — the biggest since the Great Depression. The value of most Americans' homes declined an average of 30 percent, and consumer spending dropped at least $420 billion.

About 600,000 jobs per month were lost during the year, and the unemployment rate flirted with 10 percent. A large amount of the $787 billion stimulus package was steered to social programs, and pork barrel spending was rampant. Obama persuaded Congress to approve a $3.5 trillion budget for 2010 that included a deficit of $1.2 trillion.

By late 2009, more than $60 billion had been provided in bailout financing for GM and Chrysler. The U.S. has lent, spent, or guaranteed $11.6 trillion to bolster banks since the collapse of financial institutions fueled by the failures of Freddie Mac, Fannie Mae, and AIG. Despite the dramatic downturn, many large companies continued to pay fat bonuses. Some said California's fiscal collapse was a preview of the future.

Late in the year, economists declared that the economy had hit bottom and was showing signs of a slow recovery

DICK LOCHER
Courtesy Chicago Tribune

ANGRY VILLAGERS WITH PITCHFORKS AND TORCHES!
AIG
BONUS
WHEW!
BECK ©2009

TOM BECK
Courtesy Freeport Journal-Standard (Ill.)

IT NOT ONLY MEETS THE NEW FEDERAL EMISSION STANDARDS, BUT IT SAVES MONEY ON GAS, TOO.
5-21-09
GRAHAME
© 2009 SPENCER NEWSPAPERS

NEIL GRAHAME
Courtesy Spencer Newspapers

CHRISTIAN FLEMING (ROOFUS)
Courtesy Christian Fleming.org

STORE
HELP!!
WANTED
©09 ROOFUS
WWW.CRISTIANFLEMING.ORG

AS A CITIZEN OF THE UNITED STATES...
AND ON THE ANNIVERSARY OF ONE OF MAN'S GREATEST ACHIEVEMENTS...
I BELIEVE THAT IT IS MY GOVERNMENT'S RESPONSIBILITY TO CONSIDER THE VAST EMPTINESS...
...OF MY WALLET...
HALL © 2009 ARTIZANS .com

ED HALL
Courtesy Baker County Press (Fla.)

ADAM ZYGLIS
Courtesy Buffalo News

JOSEPH RANK
Courtesy Times-Press-Recorder (Calif.)

WALT HANDELSMAN
Courtesy Newsday

ED STEIN
Courtesy Rocky Mountain News

CHARLIE DANIEL
Courtesy Knoxville News-Sentinel

JIMMY MARGULIES
Courtesy The Record (N.J.)

JAY LAMM
Courtesy Franklin Times

DEB MILBRATH
Courtesy CNN AAEC

STEVE GREENBERG
Courtesy Ventura County Star

JEFF KOTERBA
Courtesy Omaha World-Herald

NATE BEELER
Courtesy Washington Examiner

STEVE MCBRIDE
Courtesy The Reporter (Kan.)

ROB SMITH JR.
Courtesy DBR Media

JERRY GARDEN
Courtesy Garden ARToons

MICHAEL OSBUN
Courtesy Citrus City
Chronicle (Fla.)

BILL SMITH and LYNN CARLSON
Courtesy Lompoc Record

SCOTT STANTIS
Courtesy Birmingham News

JESSE SPRINGER
Courtesy Eugene Register-Guard

DEREGULATION WAS STARTED UNDER REAGAN
FINALLY, HE DEFEATED BOTH COMMUNISM AND CAPITALISM!
NEW YORK

GUY BADEAUX
Courtesy Le Droit (Canada)

PUTTING UP A BRAVE FRONT THIS CHRISTMAS, DESPITE THE ECONOMY

SCOTT COFFMAN
Courtesy Scott Coffman

TOM STIGLICH
Courtesy Northeast Times (Pa.)

Tom Stiglich©2008
WWW.TOMSTIGLICH.COM
I LOVE CONFETTI!!!
THEY'RE LAYOFF NOTICES.
2009

IT'S A CREDIT CARD OFFER. I'VE BEEN PRE-APPROVED FOR $30,000.
VIC HARVILLE
©STEPHENS MEDIA 5/15/09

VIC HARVILLE
Courtesy Stephens Media

WAYNE STROOT
Courtesy Hastings Tribune (Neb.)

WE SEEM TO BE GAINING SPEED!
DON'T BLAME ME... IT WAS GOING IN THIS DIRECTION WHEN I GOT ON.
FEEL FREE TO STOP IT BEFORE WE HIT BOTTOM.
STOCK MARKET
B.O.
EMPLOYMENT NUMBERS
ECONOMY
©'09 STROOT
THE HASTINGS TRIBUNE

McBride © '09
Reporter
All that's in here are these worthless U.S. DOLLARS!
according to the Secretary of Treasury
TRASH

STEVE MCBRIDE
Courtesy The Reporter (Kan.)

KEVIN KALLAUGHER (KAL)
Courtesy The Economist,
Kaltoons.com

GREED WAS A FACTOR IN IGNITING THE GLOBAL ECONOMIC CRISIS...
MONEY!
MONEY!
MONEY!
MONEY!!
MONEY!
MONEY!
BUT FEAR NOT... CONGRESS'S STIMULUS PLAN WILL CHANGE THINGS...
MONEY!
MONEY!
MONEY!
MONEY!
Money!
MONEY
MONEY
MONEY!
WAA HOO!!
KAL 2009
The Economist

BECKOM © 09
THE PRESIDENT SAID HE WAS GONNA BRING US ALL TOGETHER . . .
. . . IT APPEARS THE MEETING PLACE WILL STAY THE SAME
UNEMPLOYMENT OFFIC

MIKE BECKOM
Courtesy Mike Beckom

JERRY BARNETT
Courtesy Boonville Standard (Ind.)

HOMELESS BLVD.
HERE'S A $MILLION FOR EACH OF YOU! ...GO BUY A HOME AND HELP OUR ECONOMY!
DISTRIBUTE THE WEALTH!
STREET PEOPLE NEED BAILOUT!
HELP!
PREZ
U.S. TREASURY
EVERYONE LOVES A CHEERFUL GIVER!
RAT BAILOUT
BARNETT

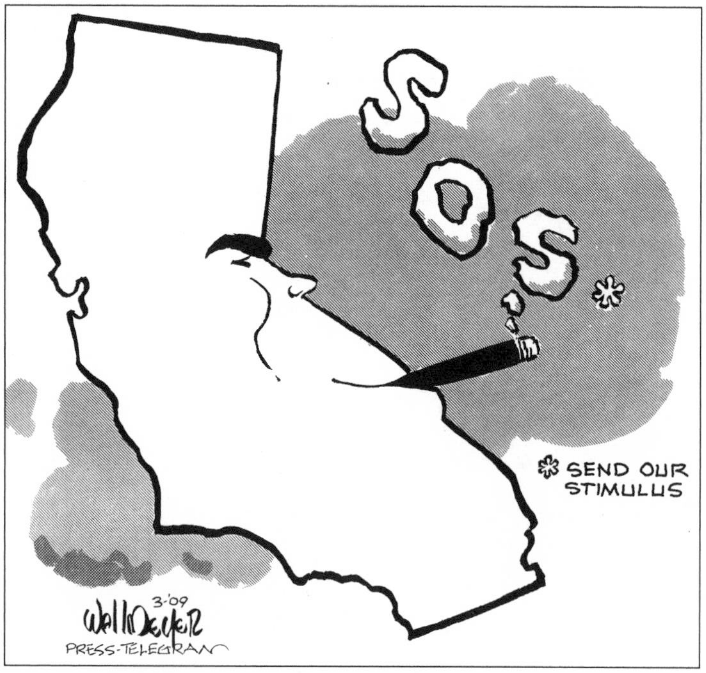
S O S *
* SEND OUR STIMULUS
3-'09
PRESS-TELEGRAM

RICHARD WALLMEYER
Courtesy Long Beach
Press-Telegram (Calif.)

WALL ST

GUY BADEAUX
Courtesy Le Droit (Canada)

Merrill Lynch Gives Mr. Thain Ultimate Addition to Luxury Office - a Private Elevator!
DANZIGER
NYTS/CWS Jan 23 09 (3873)

JEFF DANZIGER
Courtesy NYTS/CWS

The Winter of Our Discontent

COULD YOU JUST FORECLOSE ON THE REST OF THE HOUSE? WE'RE ONLY LIVING IN THE KITCHEN.
DANZIGER
NYTS/CWS Feb 18 09 (3904)

JEFF DANZIGER
Courtesy NYTS/CWS

DOUG MACGREGOR
Courtesy The News-Press (Fla.)

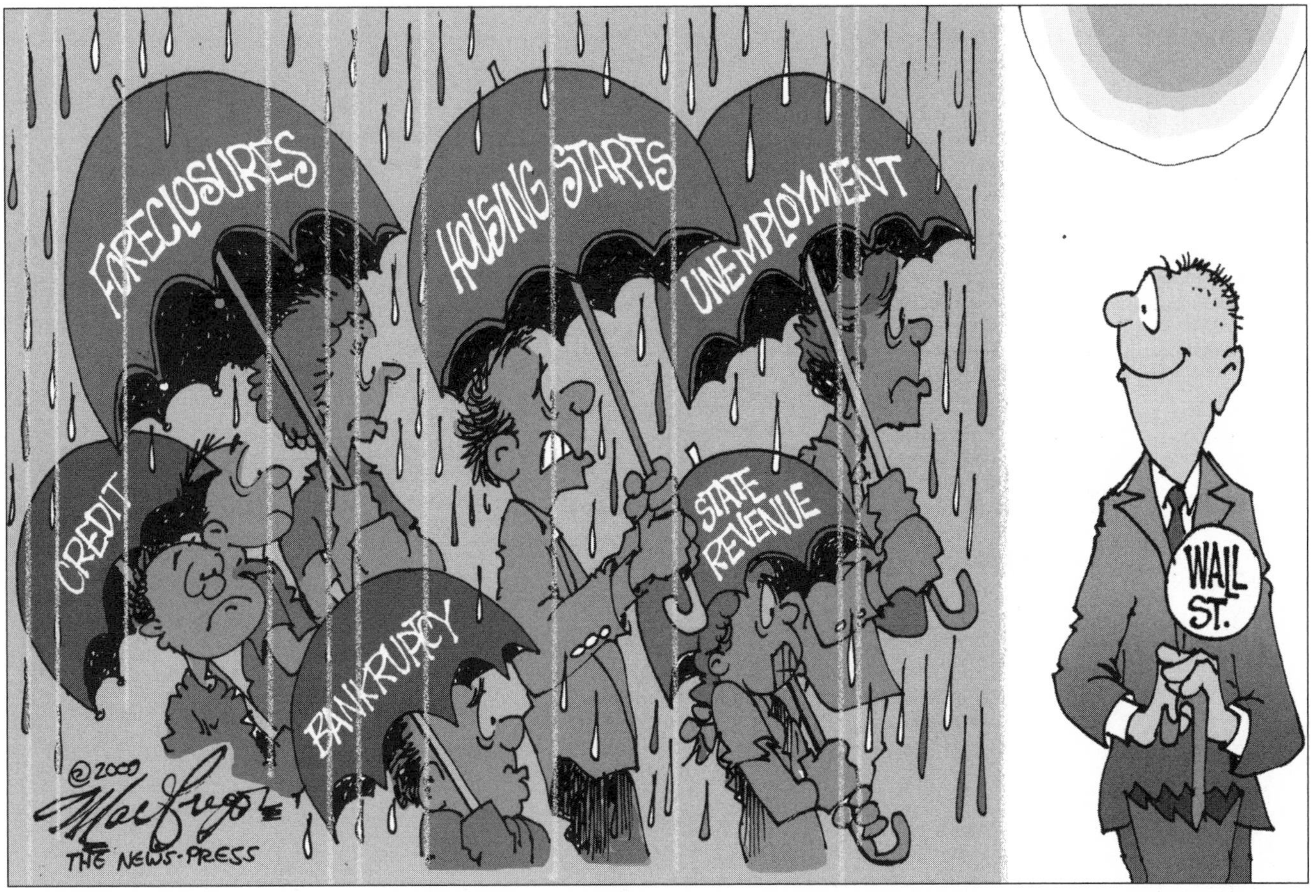

CHARLIE HALL
Courtesy Rhode Island News Group

JAY LAMM
Courtesy Franklin Times

CHAN LOWE
Courtesy South Florida Sun-Sentinel

STEPHEN TEMPLETON
Courtesy Flathead Beacon

JESSE SPRINGER
Courtesy Eugene Register-Guard

LOOKS LIKE THE GAP BETWEEN THE RICH AND THE POOR IS GETTING SHORTER AFTER ALL...
HELP
HELP
©2009 GRASDAL vueweekly

JAMES GRASDAL
Courtesy Vue Weekly

DAVID G. BROWN
Courtesy David G. Brown Studios

AIG
BONUSES
TAX PAYERS
©2009 DAVID G. BROWN STUDIOS
WWW.DAVIDGBROWN.NET
2009

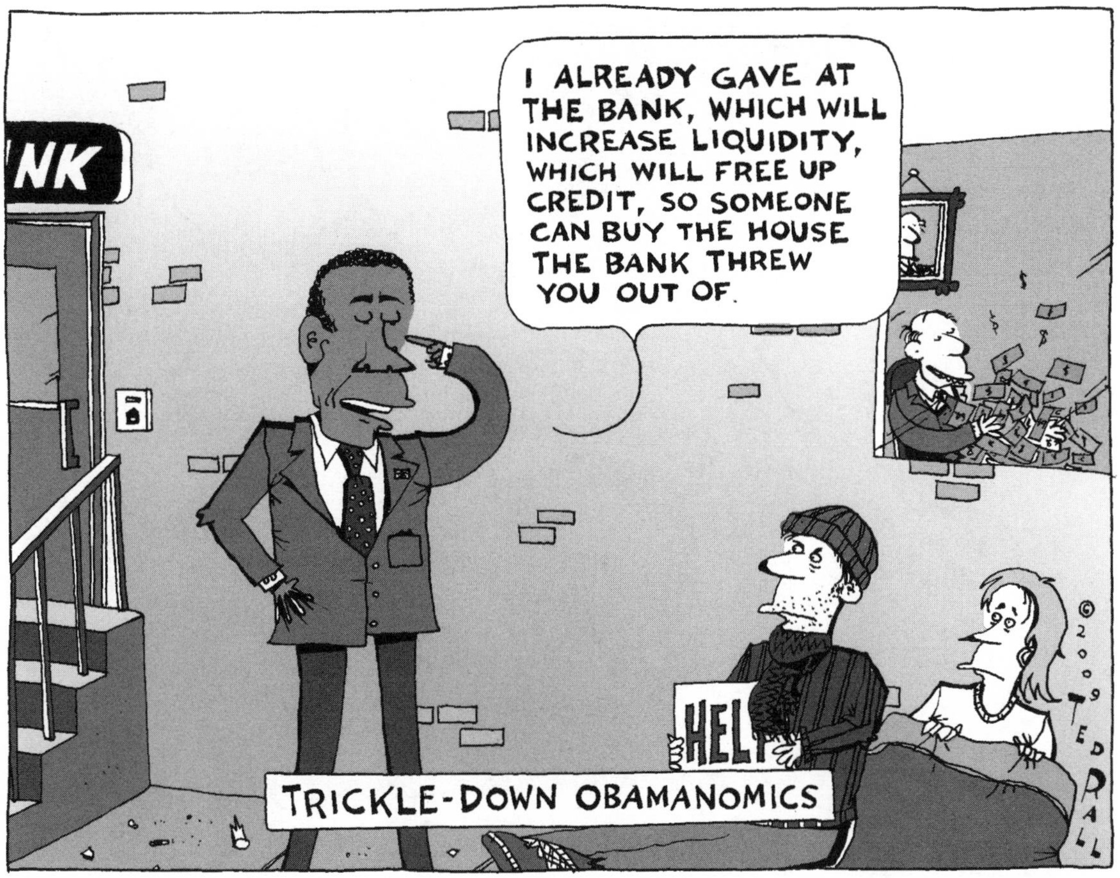
I ALREADY GAVE AT THE BANK, WHICH WILL INCREASE LIQUIDITY, WHICH WILL FREE UP CREDIT, SO SOMEONE CAN BUY THE HOUSE THE BANK THREW YOU OUT OF.
HELP
TRICKLE-DOWN OBAMANOMICS
©2009 TED RALL

TED RALL
Courtesy Universal Press Syndicate

ANNETTE BALESTERI
Courtesy Antioch News (Calif.)

The small changes in our usage... have paid off in a "No Fine" water bill.
Conserve
Sun Tea
BALESTERI – 2009
The News

2009© CREATORS.COM
GARY MARKSTEIN
IT'S MOVING!...
ALMOST A BUSTLE...
KINDA LIKE A TROT, EVEN...
ECONOMY
Z
ECONOMISTS

GARY MARKSTEIN
Courtesy Creators News Service

JEFF DANZIGER
Courtesy NYTS/CWS

If Baseball Players Got Paid Like Wall Streeters
HAH! I STRUCK OUT! THAT SHOULD BE GOOD FOR A BIG BONUS!
WIFFF...
MISSED THAT SUCKER! KA-CHING!
HEY! I'M OUT!
MONEY! MONEY! MONEY!
HAH! BALL FOUR!
RETENTION BONUS HERE I COME!
WAY TO GO! YOU BLEW A SIX RUN LEAD! TELL ME YOU DIDN'T DO IT FOR THE MONEY!
WELL, MAYBE A LITTLE, BUT HONESTLY, I REALLY DO SUCK AT PITCHING...
DANZIGER

Foreign Affairs

In visits overseas and in several speeches, President Obama has reached out to leaders of Muslim countries in an effort to improve U.S.-Muslim relations. Critics say his outreach comes at the expense of relations with Israel. International media had high praise for Obama, although he received little cooperation from European leaders in financial matters and in the war in Afghanistan.

Pakistan denied it shields terrorists, despite the presence of al-Qaida and the Taliban and ties to terrorist attacks on hotels in Mumbai, India. Following a long pattern, the United Nations criticized Israel for responding to rocket attacks from Palestinians. The debate over human rights goes on in Vladimir Putin's Russia where a journalist and a human rights lawyer were gunned down execution-style.

North Korea continued to provoke international concern over its nuclear program with test firings of missiles. President Mahmoud Ahmadinijad was re-elected in Iran, but opponents charged election fraud. Riots in the streets were met with harsh reprisals. Scotland stirred outrage in the U.S. by releasing from prison the only person sentenced in the 1988 bombing of a jetliner over Lockerbie. Somali pirates continued to plague shipping off the coast of Africa.

KEVIN KALLAUGHER (KAL)
Courtesy The Economist,
Kaltoons.com

CAREFULL! THE GREAT SATAN IS OPENING HIS CLAW!
AND HE IS NO DOUBT REACHING FOR OUR THROATS!!

DO YOU HAVE A CLUE WHY WE AREN'T RECEIVED WELL BY OTHER COUNTRIES?
I'VE BEEN BAFFLED BY THAT FOR SOME TIME NOW.
Welcome To Kim Jong-il's Weapons Discount
IRAN ROCKS
5-2-2009 NATIONAL FREE PRESS
MJ © 2009 PC STUDIOS

MICHAEL POHRER
Courtesy National Free Press

ED HALL
Courtesy Baker County Press (Fla.)

LARRY WRIGHT
Courtesy Detroit News

IT SCARES THE HECK OUT OF THE WEST WHEN THEY GO INTO ECONOMIC DOWNTURN AND WE SHOW OUR ROCKET MISSILES ARE AS GOOD AS THEY EVER WERE!
NORTH KOREA
©2009 LARRY WRIGHT
THE DETROIT NEWS

CHRISTIAN FLEMING (ROOFUS)
Courtesy Christian Fleming.org

You need to spend trillions on your own stimulus programs!
I don't think so!!
You need to send more combat troops to Afghanistan!
I don't think so!!
Turkey should be allowed to join the European Union!
I don't think so!
Well...how did I do?
I think you did great!
clap... clap... clap... clap... clap...
Europe
NATO
EU
World Media

ED GAMBLE
Courtesy Florida Times-Union

DAVID DONAR
Courtesy Macomb Daily (Miss.)

Donar

In Mr. Putin's Russia, the Debate on Human Rights Goes On

JEFF DANZIGER
Courtesy NYTS/CWS

JOEL PETT
Courtesy Lexington Herald-Leader

OKAY, SO I SENT YOUR SON ON A SUICIDE MISSION AND REFUSE TO EDUCATE YOUR DAUGHTER... BUT CAN YOU AFFORD TO LOSE MY TALENT?
JOEL PETT
JUSTIFYING TALIBAN EXECUTIVE PAY

SCOTT STANTIS
Courtesy Birmingham News

BOB GORRELL
Courtesy Creators Syndicate

IRAN
08/2/09 HARTFORD COURANT.

BOB ENGLEHART
Courtesy Hartford Courant

RANDY BISH
Courtesy Tribune-Review (Pa.)

KNOCK KNOCK
WHO'S THERE?
AYATOLLAH
AYATOLLAH WHO?
AYATOLLAH YOU TO STOP ASKING QUESTIONS ABOUT THE ELECTION! HAHAHA!
BANG!
BISH TRIBUNE-REVIEW

I'll miss you, Dubya...
...much like how you've kept missing me all these years!
Peterson
Vancouver Sun

ROY PETERSON
Courtesy Vancouver Sun

Hunau 09

BARRY HUNAU
Courtesy cartoonsbybarry.com

DAVID DONAR
Courtesy Macomb Daily (Miss.)

Donar

GARY MARKSTEIN
Courtesy Creators News Service

JIMMY MARGULIES
Courtesy The Record (N.J.)

The pen is mightier than the sword.
— Bulwer-Lytton (1803-1873)
DOWN WITH TYRANTS
The pda is mightier than the sword.
— Iran (2009)
COHEN ©2009

DAVID COHEN
Courtesy Ashville Citizen-Times

DAVID FITZSIMMONS
Courtesy Arizona Daily Star

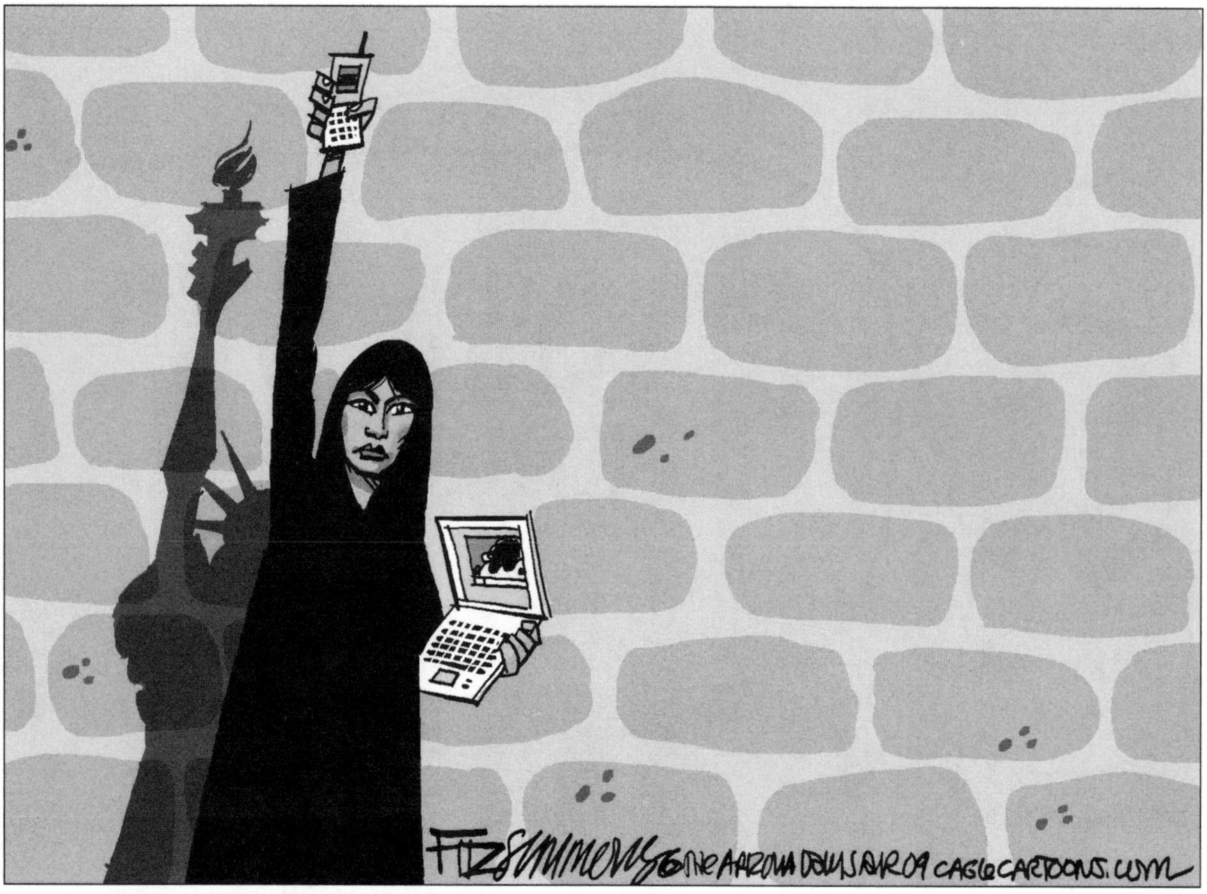
FITZSIMMONS

ABDEL BASSET ALI AL-MEGRAHI
I SURVIVED THE LOCKERBIE CRASH
GADHAFI
©2009 SUMMERS ORLANDOSENTINEL

DANA SUMMERS
Courtesy Orlando Sentinel

MICHAEL RAMIREZ
Courtesy Investors Business Daily

RAMIREZ INVESTOR'S BUSINESS DAILY 2009© CREATORS.COM
NORTH KOREA
RESERVED for our DEAR LEADER
I'M OUT OF TOILET PAPER. QUICK, GRAB ANOTHER U.S. HOSTAGE.

Sorry... not enough room for everyone!
ROAD MAP to PEACE in The MIDDLE EAST
ISRAEL
OBAMA Peace Tour
McBride © '09 Reporter

STEVE MCBRIDE
Courtesy The Reporter (Kan.)

GAZA

CHUCK LEGGE
Courtesy The Frontiersman

STEVE RUSTAD
Courtesy petaluma360.com

THE UNITED NATIONS ADMONISHES ISRAEL FOR ITS NAKED AGGRESSION AGAINST A HELPLESS NEIGHBOR STATE. FOR THE RECORD, WE CONSIDER THE PALESTINIAN ROCKETS THAT RAIN DOWN ON YOUR CIVILIANS A LEGITIMATE FORM OF POLITICAL PROTEST.
UN
ISRAEL
HTTP://STEVE-RUSTAD.PETALUMA360.COM

Yo, ho, ho
and a tanker
of oil
-EVANS-
©'08

PETER EVANS
Courtesy Islander News (Fla.)

RANAN LURIE
Courtesy Cartoonews, Inc.

HUNGER
GLOBAL WARMING
GENOCIDE
LURIE
U.N.Secretary General Ban Ki-moon's Explosive Future
2009 INTERNATIONAL COPYRIGHT BY CARTOONEWS INC., N.Y.C., USA

I'M NOT TOUCHING YOU!... I'M NOT TOUCHING YOU!.... I'M NOT TOUCHING YOU!...
JUST TRY IT,...PUNK!
KIM
N. KOREA

JOE GROSHEK
Courtesy Joe Groshek

MARTY RISKIN
Courtesy Penspeakcartoons.com

TURNING OVER IN THEIR GRAVES...
LOCKERBIE VICTIMS
BOMBER FREED!

Media/Entertainment

Most of the mainstream electronic and print media have been accused of bias in favor of President Obama from the time he entered the national political scene. Obama was criticized for appearing on the Jay Leno Show. Critics said it undermines the dignity of the office.

Across the nation, more and more newspapers faced difficult financial times. Often, editorial cartoonists are the first to feel the pinch as newspapers downsize. Competition from the electronic media, especially the internet, has speeded the demise of newspapers. Faced with competition from free internet sites, many newspapers have put their content on the internet as well. Fox News bills its programming as "fair and balanced," but left-leaning partisans call it too right-wing. Obama singled out Fox News as being unfairly critical of his administration.

Fox News' Glenn Beck gained a large following from conservatives and independents who are concerned that liberals are pushing the U.S. toward socialism. Conservative talk radio giant Rush Limbaugh, a thorn in the side of liberals, was accused of various misdeeds, including "spewing hate speech."

Walt Disney Co. acquired Marvel Entertainment for $4 billion.

JUSTIN DeFREITAS
Courtesy Berkeley Daily Planet

Times In Danger
Tribune is Bankrupt
The squeeze is on for No. 2 papers
©2009 RooFus

CHRISTIAN FLEMING (ROOFUS)
Courtesy Christian Fleming.org

I RESIGN.
PLEASE TELL ME THAT'S TINA FEY !
SARAH PALIN

J.R. ROSE
Courtesy Byrd Newspapers

RICK MCKEE
Courtesy Augusta Chronicle

NEWS Then
...and THAT'S the WAY IT IS....
LIKE YOUR TRUSTWORTHY UNCLE
NEWS Now
24 HOURS
...NEXT UP: MICHAEL JACKSON'S DERMATOLOGIST'S PET PSYCHIC!
LIKE YOUR CRAZY AUNT

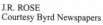

STEPHEN TEMPLETON
Courtesy Flathead Beacon

JOHN SHERFFIUS
Courtesy Boulder Camera

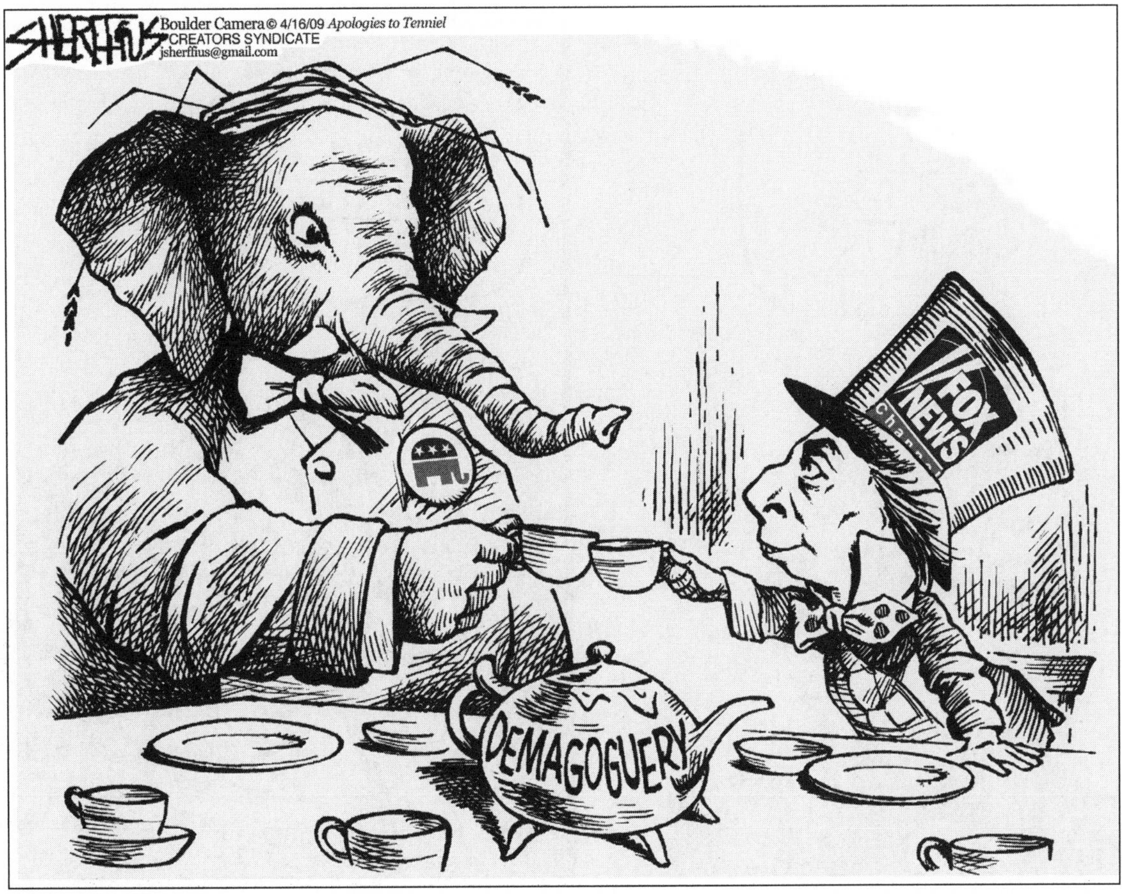

2009 © FULLER
ARTIZANS.COM
WOW, MICHELLE, YOU REALLY WANT TO MAKE PASSIONATE LOVE ON OUR FIRST NIGHT IN THE WHITE HOUSE? HOW ROMANTIC!
ACTUALLY, THAT WAS ME!....
Media

JOHN FULLER
Courtesy Artizans.com

STEVE BREEN
Courtesy San Diego Union-Tribune

WE'LL FIX THE COUNTRY...
OBAMA
BIDEN
WE'LL FIX THE ELECTION.
abc
TIME
POST
The New York Times
CNN
STUDY: MEDIA BIAS FAVORS OBAMA

ROY PETERSON
Courtesy Vancouver Sun

DAVID FITZSIMMONS
Courtesy Arizona Daily Star

McCLOSKEY
Rush

JIM MCCLOSKEY
Courtesy The News-Leader (Va.)

GLENN BECK HERE, FANNING THE FLAMES OF DEMOCRACY!
FOX
HUFFAKER
POLITICALCARTOONS.COM

SANDY HUFFAKER
Courtesy politicalcartoons.com

CHUCK LEGGE
Courtesy The Frontiersman

PRESS ROOM
YOU MEAN IT'S NOT A TANNING BED?
FRONTIERSMAN 2009

I'm a journalist.
Hey, me too.
I'm a reporter. My paper is dying.
My blog gets forty million hits a day.
This is my latest story. It took weeks of research, travel, interviews, secret sources, personal expenses, and risks to my family. How did you write yours?
I googled and copied your story, posted a link, and added a snide remark.--Hey, look! I just got named 'Blogger of the year.'
But THAT's not JOURNALISM! Name ONE DIFFERENCE between MY STORY and the one on your BLOG!
That's easy: My story is free.
But it wasn't "free" to ME!
Parasite.
Dinosaur.
2/27/09 Steve Edwards. St. Louis Journalism Review © Edwards
EdwardsCartoon@yahoo.com

STEVE EDWARDS
Courtesy St. Louis Journalism Review

MILT PRIGGEE
Courtesy Puget Sound
Business Journal

FREE NEWSPAPER WEBSITE ACCESS
PRIGGEE ©09-2
www.MILTPRIGGEE.com

GLOOM
WHY SO GLOOMY?
MEDIA
CONSUMER
DULUTH NEWS TRIBUNE 1-09

STEVE LINDSTROM
Courtesy Duluth News-Tribune

LOOK AT THAT! ANOTHER NEWSPAPER CLOSING!
STAHLER.
www.comics.com
3/24
© 2009 Jeff Stahler/ Dist. by NEA, Inc.

JEFF STAHLER
Courtesy NEA

TIM JACKSON
Courtesy Chicago Defender

News Item:
The Walt Disney Co. to acquire Marvel Entertainment, Inc. in $4 billion deal!
Ew— WHAT THIS HULK STEP IN?
©
Tim Jackson
2009
090831
obita@cistoons.com
(The Amazing Spider-man & The Incredible Hulk likenesses © Marvel Comics.
Mickey Mouse & Donald Duck likenesses © Walt Disney Co.)

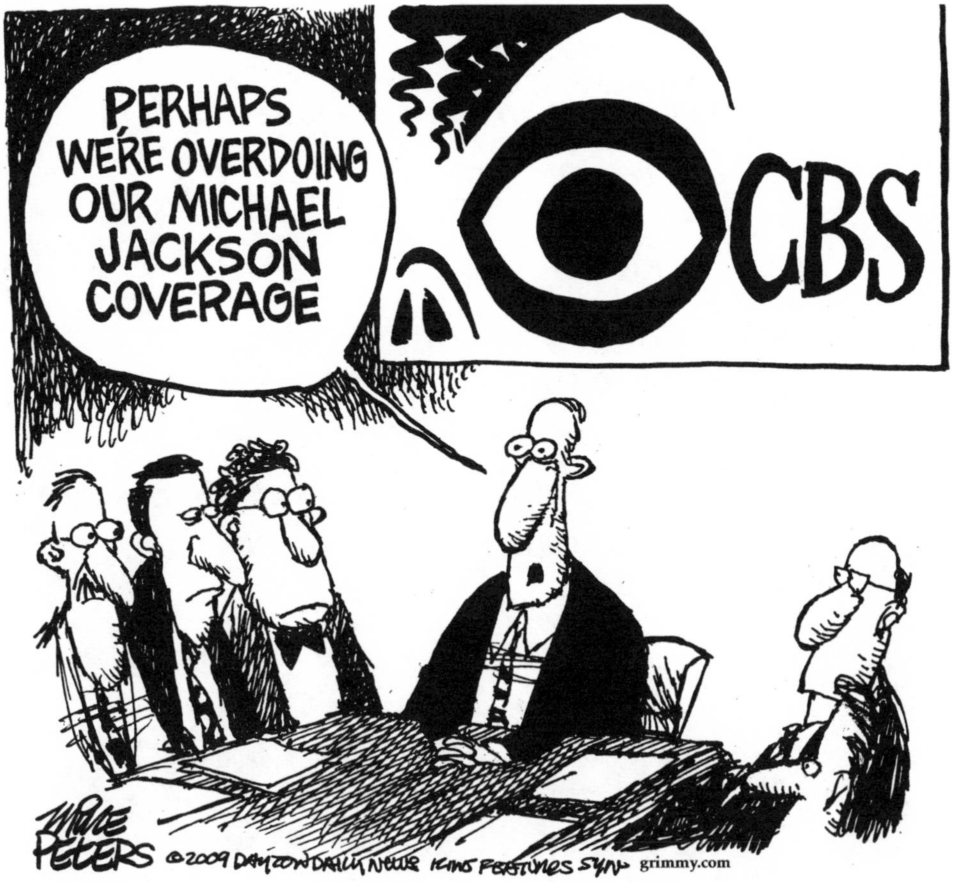
PERHAPS WE'RE OVERDOING OUR MICHAEL JACKSON COVERAGE
CBS
MIKE PETERS ©2009 DAYTON DAILY NEWS KING FEATURES SYN
grimmy.com

MIKE PETERS
Courtesy Dayton Daily News

AUGUST J. POLLAK
Courtesy August J. Pollak

AS SOME OF YOU HEARD, BILL DONOHUE'S CATHOLIC LEAGUE HAS DEMANDED A DISCLAIMER APPEAR IN THE NEW "DA VINCI CODE" SEQUEL SAYING IT'S NOT TRUE.*
UNFORTUNATELY, IN A DEAL WITH THE MOVIE STUDIO, I AM NOW OBLIGATED TO ALERT YOU IN ADVANCE THAT THE FOLLOWING STORY YOU'RE ABOUT TO HEAR IS ALSO BASED ON A WORK OF FICTION THAT MAY BE INSPIRED BY ACTUAL EVENTS, ALTHOUGH CHARACTERS HAVE BEEN ALTERED FROM REAL LIFE FOR ARTISTIC PURPOSES.
* TRUE.
POLLAK

I MAKE A MOTION THAT WE AMEND OUR BY-LAWS SO THAT PEOPLE WHO DON'T EARN 100% OF THEIR INCOME DRAWING CARTOONS FULL TIME FOR A DAILY NEWSPAPER– CAN STILL BE A REGULAR MEMBER!
obita@cistoons.com
© Tim Jackson 2009
090629

TIM JACKSON
Courtesy Chicago Defender

MILT PRIGGEE
Courtesy Puget Sound
Business Journal

I GUESS BEN FRANKLIN WAS RIGHT WHEN HE SAID THE SMALLEST LEAK WILL SINK THE LARGEST SHIP...
I TOLD YA WE SHOULDN'T HAVE FIRED OUR EDITORIAL CARTOONIST.
THE DAILY-TRIBUNE-NEWS-HERALD-REPORTER-JOURNAL GLOBE-RECORD-INDEPENDENT-MESSENGER-STANDARD MIRROR-PRESS-GAZETTE-EXPRESS-ADVOCATE-POST CHRONICLE-REVIEW-TIMES-SUN-STAR and MAIL
HAPPY NATIONAL CARTOONISTS DAY!
PRIGGEE ©09-5 WWW.MILTPRIGGEE.com

A RECESSION IS THE PERFECT TIME TO UPDATE YOUR JOB SKILLS
MACKAY
HAMILTON SPECTATOR
OW!

GRAEME MACKAY
Courtesy Hamilton Spectator (Can.)

MIKE PETERS
Courtesy Dayton Daily News

HE DID THE LENO SHOW LAST NIGHT.
MIKE PETERS
©2009 DAYTON DAILY NEWS KING FEATURES
grimmy.com

JEFF DANZIGER
Courtesy NYTS/CWS

MIKE KEEFE
Courtesy Denver Post

The Military

Following up on his campaign promises, President Obama set about winding down the war in Iraq and sent more troops to Afghanistan. The dispatch of 17,000 additional troops fulfilled a longstanding request by commander of U.S. forces in Afghanistan David D. McKiernan, who was later dismissed.

The military situation continued to deteriorate, and in September top commanders called for even more troops. Today's debate echoes that which preceded the successful surge in Iraq three years ago, but this time there is more consensus within the military. The thorny problem for U.S. troops in Afghanistan is how to combat Taliban fighters and at the same time keep civilian casualties to a minimum.

Obama adopted a strategy of focusing on efforts to win over the civilian population, a move long sought by commanders on the ground. The conflict has become less an international effort, as European allies seem to have lost interest. Monthly troop casualties now surpass U.S. losses in Iraq.

A memo from the U.S. Department of Homeland Security warned that soldiers returning from Iraq and Afghanistan could be radicalized by right-wing extremists. The missive sparked outrage among many Americans.

DENNIS DRAUGHON
Courtesy The Insider (N.C.)

THE TERRORIST, THE HUMAN SHIELD, AND THE SOLDIER
I AM PREPARED AND WILLING TO DIE FOR MY BELIEFS!
I AM PREPARED AND WILLING TO DIE FOR MY BELIEFS!
WAR NO MORE
I AM PREPARED AND WILLING TO LET THEM.
©Mark Baker 2009

MARK BAKER
Courtesy Army Times

DO YOU REMEMBER THOSE "HUMAN SHIELD" PEOPLE?
Yeah. WHAT EVER HAPPEND WITH THEM?
©Mark Baker 2009

MARK BAKER
Courtesy Army Times

CHAN LOWE
Courtesy South Florida Sun-Sentinel

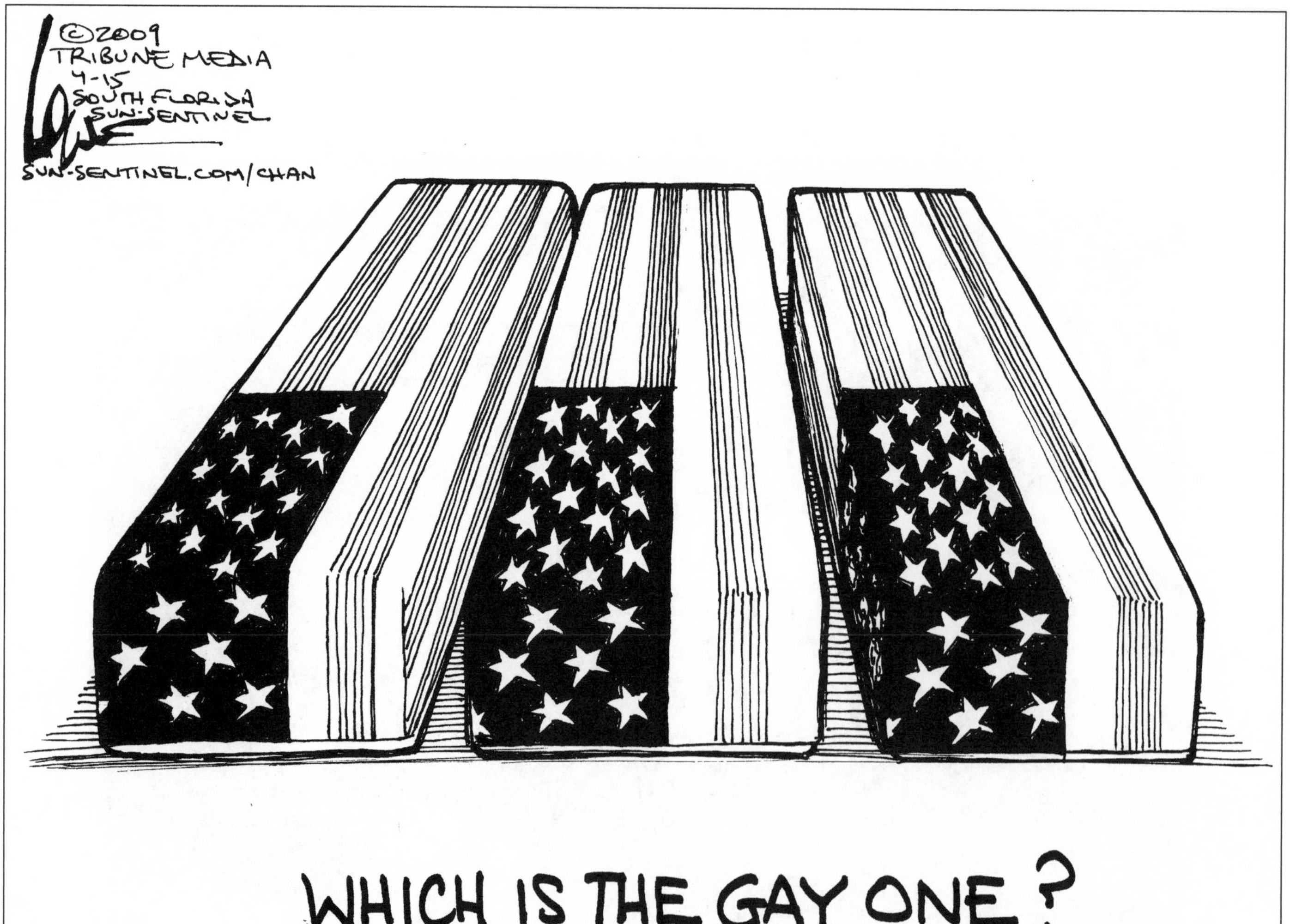
©2009 TRIBUNE MEDIA
4-15
SOUTH FLORIDA SUN-SENTINEL
SUN-SENTINEL.COM/CHAN
WHICH IS THE GAY ONE?

POL GALVEZ
Courtesy Philippine News

ED GAMBLE
Courtesy Florida Times-Union

McCLOSKEY
THE REPORTS OF MY DEMISE ARE GREATLY EXAGGERATED!
U.S. Military
Somali Pirates

JIM MCCLOSKEY
Courtesy The News-Leader (Va.)

EUGENE PAYNE
Courtesy Charlotte Observer

THERE ARE THOSE WHO KNOW HOW TO FIGHT A WAR...
AND THERE ARE THOSE WHO HAVEN'T A CLUE!
PAYNE

THIS IS MY UNCLE JAMES. HE IS A DECORATED WAR HERO WHO FOUGHT IN IRAQ. ...OH, AND HE'S GAY...
TODAY
Ask 'n' tell
COHEN ©2009

DAVID COHEN
Courtesy Ashville Citizen-Times

STEVE RUSTAD
Courtesy petaluma360.com

YES, WE'RE SENDING YOU INTO AFGHANISTAN BUT ONLY WITH THE PROVISO THAT YOU DON'T DO ANYTHING RISKY. JUST BECAUSE THIS "COMBAT" THING WORKED OUT IN IRAQ DOESN'T MEAN THAT AMERICA'S POLITICAL ESTABLISHMENT HAS THE...DESIRE...TO SUPPORT MORE SHOOTING OR BLOWING THINGS UP. OF COURSE, I KNOW THAT YOU AND THE OTHER SOLDIERS ARE TRAINED TO DO THAT SORT OF THING, BUT WE CA LY AUTHORIZE YOUR TAKING ANY KIND OF FENSIZE ACTION IF IT POSES NO RISK TO PERSON - THE ENEMY NOT WITHSTANDI ND WHILE I'M ON THE SUBJECT I THINK WE D TO BE EXTREMELY CAREFUL WHO WE LABEL THE "ENEMY," AFTER ALL IN 20 OR YEARS THOSE FOLKS MAY WELL BE OUR ALLIES AND WE WOULDN'T WANT TO LEAVE ANY BAD FEELINGS THAT MIGHT PREVENT US FROM SELLING THEM WEAPONS AND STUFF...
STATE DEPT. OF RISK PREVENTION
HTTP://STEVE-RUSTAD.PETALUMA360.COM
RUSTAD

...REMEMBER THE GLORY DAYS OF BASEBALL, WHEN HAVING A CASE OF 'ROIDS' JUST MEANT ANAL DISCOMFORT...

BRUCE MACKINNON
Courtesy Halifax Herald (Can.)

MIKE LUCKOVICH
Courtesy Atlanta Journal-Constitution

MIKE LUCKOVICH
ATLANTA JOURNAL-CONSTITUTION
AJC.com 2-13-9
HANK AARON
HOW COME WHEN WE TAKE STEROIDS, HE GETS BIGGER?...
Clemens
A-ROD
BONDS
McGWIRE

Sports

Atlanta Falcons quarterback Michael Vick was sentenced to 18 months in prison for his involvement in an illegal dog-fighting ring. Upon his release in mid-2009, he signed with the Philadelphia Eagles and soon was back on the playing field.

Brett Favre, longtime quarterback for the Green Bay Packers, announced his retirement in 2008, but soon reconsidered and was traded to the New York Jets. In February of 2009, Favre told the New York Jets that he was again retiring. He changed his mind a second time and in August signed with the Minnesota Vikings. Some in the sports world claimed his legacy as a football player had become overshadowed by his need for attention.

Widespread use of steroids in professional sports has called many sports records into question. In early 2009, Olympic swimming star Michael Phelps admitted to "behavior which was regrettable" and said he had demonstrated bad judgment after a photo surfaced in a British tabloid, showing him using a bong, a device used for smoking marijuana. Phelps was not prosecuted in connection with the incident.

Legendary coach Bobby Knight was inducted into the Indiana Basketball Hall of Fame.

TIM BENSON
Courtesy Argus Leader (S.D.)

LET VICK PLAY FOOTBALL AGAIN BY THE SAME RULES HE GAVE US...
YOU LOSE YOU GET THE CENSORED BEAT OUT OF YOU!
YOU WIN YOU GET THE CENSORED BEAT OUT OF YOU.
BOILEAU THE STATE JOURNAL 2009

LINDA BOILEAU
Courtesy Frankfort State Journal (Ky.)

VICK TO SPEND TWO MONTHS UNDER HOUSE ARREST...
...with apologies to Schulz...
COHEN ©2009

DAVID COHEN
Courtesy Ashville Citizen-Times

RANDY BISH
Courtesy Tribune-Review (Pa.)

BISH TRIBUNE REVIEW
VICK
HONEY, HAVE YOU SEEN MY NEW EAGLES JERSEY?

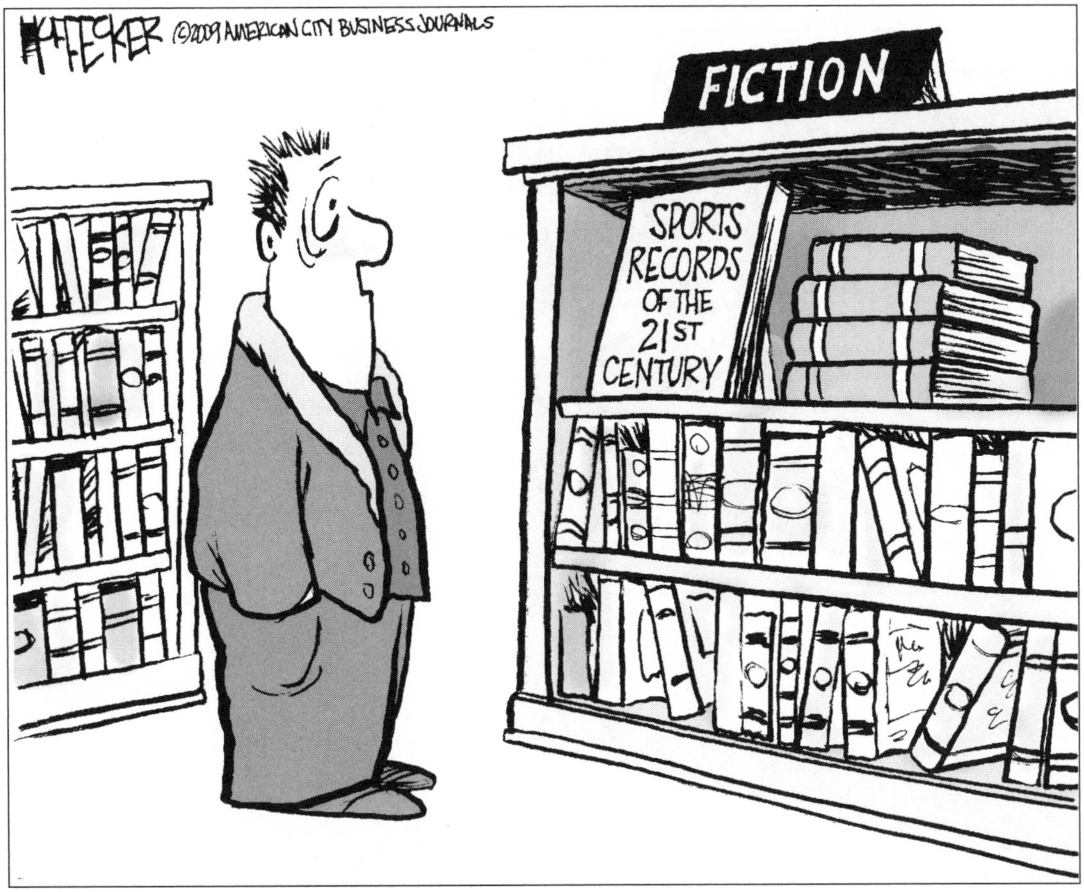

JOSEPH HOFFECKER
Courtesy American City Business Journals

TOM STIGLICH
Courtesy Northeast Times (Pa.)

SHOW UP AND THROW SOME CHAIRS AT THEM!
TO FORGIVE IS DEVINE!
IU TO HONOR BOB KNIGHT!
HALL of FAME
BARNETT

JERRY BARNETT
Courtesy Boonville Standard (Ind.)

Hey, it's just Manny being Manny sticking fanny
MANNY
Wonder who his GYN is...
ESTROGEN
LA
Charlie Hall

CHARLIE HALL
Courtesy Rhode Island News Group

DAVID DONAR
Courtesy Macomb Daily (Miss.)

NY
AROD
BONDS
PHELPS
Donar

MICHAEL VICK SIGNS WITH THE EAGLES
NOW LEAVING PHILADELPHIA

CHRIS BRITT
Courtesy State Journal-Register (Ill.)

STEVE KELLEY
Courtesy The Times Picayune (La.)

IT WON'T BE EASY GETTING HIRED.
VICK
WHAT I NEED IS A LEG UP.
THE TIMES-PICAYUNE © 2009
S. KELLEY

TIM BENSON
Courtesy Argus Leader (S.D.)

JOE HELLER
Courtesy Green Bay Press & Gazette

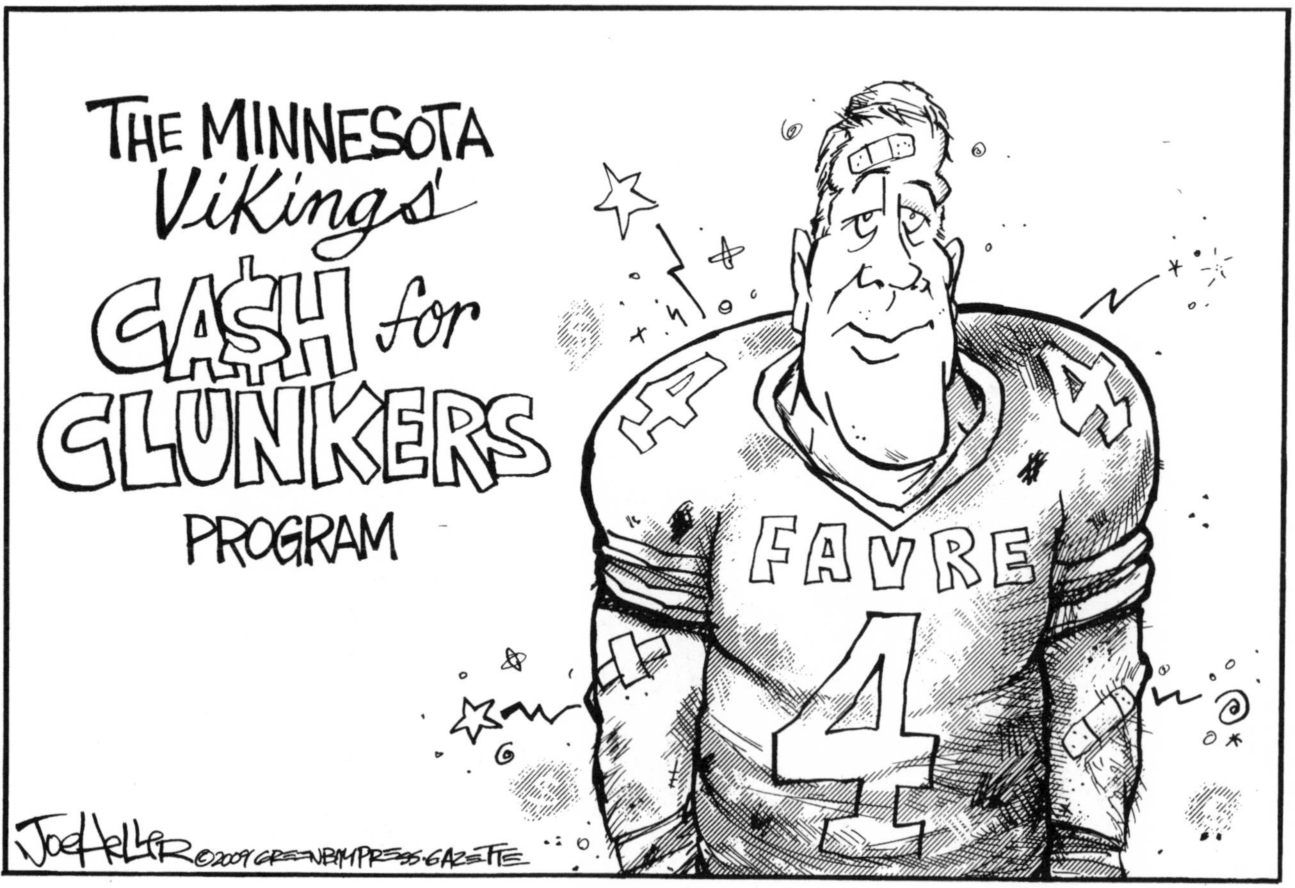

Canada

Canada has figured prominently in the U.S. debate over health care reform. Many Canadians, tired of waiting for medical care at home, cross the border for treatment in the U.S. Some Canadians worry that if the U.S. adopts a system similar to their own, they may have nowhere to go to get the treatment they need.

Meeting with Canadian Prime Minister Stephen Harper, President Obama warned against a "strong impulse" toward protectionism while the world suffers a global economic recession and said efforts to renegotiate NAFTA will have to wait. In August, President Obama held talks with Harper and Mexican President Felipe Calderon in Guadalajara, Mexico. The talks centered upon the economy, drug violence, and the environment.

The new leader of the Liberal opposition, Michael Ignatieff ("Iggy"), was formally introduced to the world at the Liberal Party convention in Vancouver. Ignatieff was portrayed as a dynamic new force on the political scene.

A United Kingdom charity advised parents not to allow their children to eat processed ham. The World Cancer Research Fund UK announced that if children consume too much processed meat they are more likely to develop bowel cancer.

LISA BENSON
Courtesy Washington Post Writers Group

YOU, SIR... YOU HAVE A QUESTION?
Dist. by Wash.Post Writers Group
Lisa ©2009 8-19
WILL I BE ABLE TO KEEP MY DOCTOR?
CANADA

AS A CANADIAN MR. BAY, WHO MOST INSPIRED YOU TO BECOME AN AMERICAN CITIZEN?
MY U.S. DOCTOR.
SOX

WILLIAM O'TOOLE
Courtesy oppositepicks.net

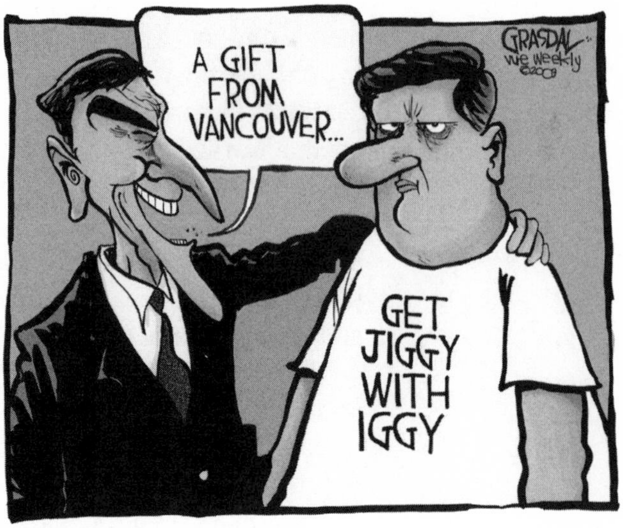
A GIFT FROM VANCOUVER...
GET JIGGY WITH IGGY

JAMES GRASDAL
Courtesy Vue Weekly

STEVE NEASE
Courtesy Toronto Sun

HAPPY YEAR OF THE OX...
BUDGET
DEFICIT

ROY PETERSON
Courtesy Vancouver Sun

BUY
NORTH
AMERICAN !
NAFTA

IS THAT A CRYBABY I HEAR TALKING PROTECTIONISM?
CANADA
U.S.A.

THEO MOUDAKIS
Courtesy Toronto Star

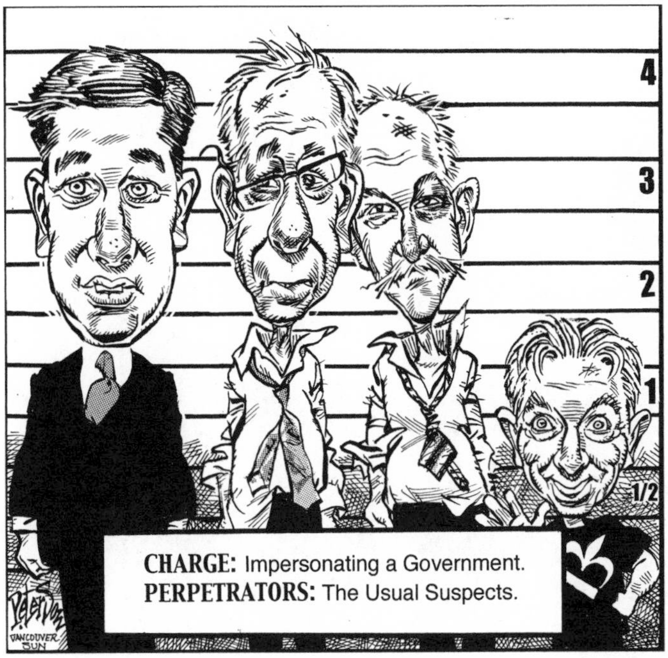
4
3
2
1
1/2
CHARGE: Impersonating a Government.
PERPETRATORS: The Usual Suspects.

ROY PETERSON
Courtesy Vancouver Sun

NEASE '09
YOU'RE THE HOST, YOU BRING UP PROTECTIONISM...
BUY AMERICAN
3 AMIGOS SUMMIT

STEVE NEASE
Courtesy Toronto Sun

JAMES GRASDAL
Courtesy Vue Weekly

FRED CURATOLO
Courtesy Edmonton Sun

. . . and Other Issues

A U.S. Airways plane with 155 people aboard ditched in a chilly Hudson River after striking a flock of birds upon takeoff from New York's LaGuardia Airport. Everyone on board survived. The pilot, Chesley B. "Sully" Sullenberger, emerged as a hero. Sonia Maria Sotomayor was sworn in as the U.S. Supreme Court's first Hispanic justice.

Many people who had never before been involved in politics showed up at town hall meetings across the country to voice their opposition to government-run health care, spending, and high taxes. California's economy plunged into crisis, with 11.5 percent unemployment and spiraling debt. Former Vice President Dick Cheney defended the Bush administration's policies, declaring "they kept us safe."

Historic swindler Bernard Madoff was sentenced to 150 years in prison for massive fraud, and gasoline prices fluctuated widely. Buoyed by President Obama, unions seemed to be feeling their oats. Barbie, the iconic doll, turned 50.

Notables who died in 2009 included Sen. Ted Kennedy, pop star Michael Jackson, actress Farrah Fawcett, newsman Walter Cronkite, Johnny Carson's former sidekick Ed McMahon, and radio commentator Paul Harvey.

MIKE LUCKOVICH
Courtesy Atlanta Journal-Constitution

YOU'RE TELLING ME SHE'S 50?!
SHE HAS SO HAD WORK DONE...
Barbie
NEASE '09

STEVE NEASE
Courtesy Toronto Sun

IS IT OK TO REGISTER VOTERS BORN IN 1859?
RIP
RIP 1859-1921
RIP 1880-1950
RIP 1905-1980
ACORN? HEY-ITS A NEW JERSEY TRADITION TOO
WALTER LIEBERMAN GIEB

WALTER LIEBERMAN
Courtesy Walter Lieberman

JIM BUSH
Courtesy Providence Journal (R.I.)

DANI AGUILA
Courtesy Filipino Reporter

JOHN SHERFFIUS
Courtesy Boulder Camera

©09 Daytona Beach News-Journal
Creators News Service
BEATTIE
SOTOMAYOR
"I think it's great you'll bring some empathy to the court.
Take this and give it to one of the other justices."

BRUCE BEATTIE
Courtesy Daytona Beach News-Journal

ROSS GOSSE
Courtesy EDITOONS, inck

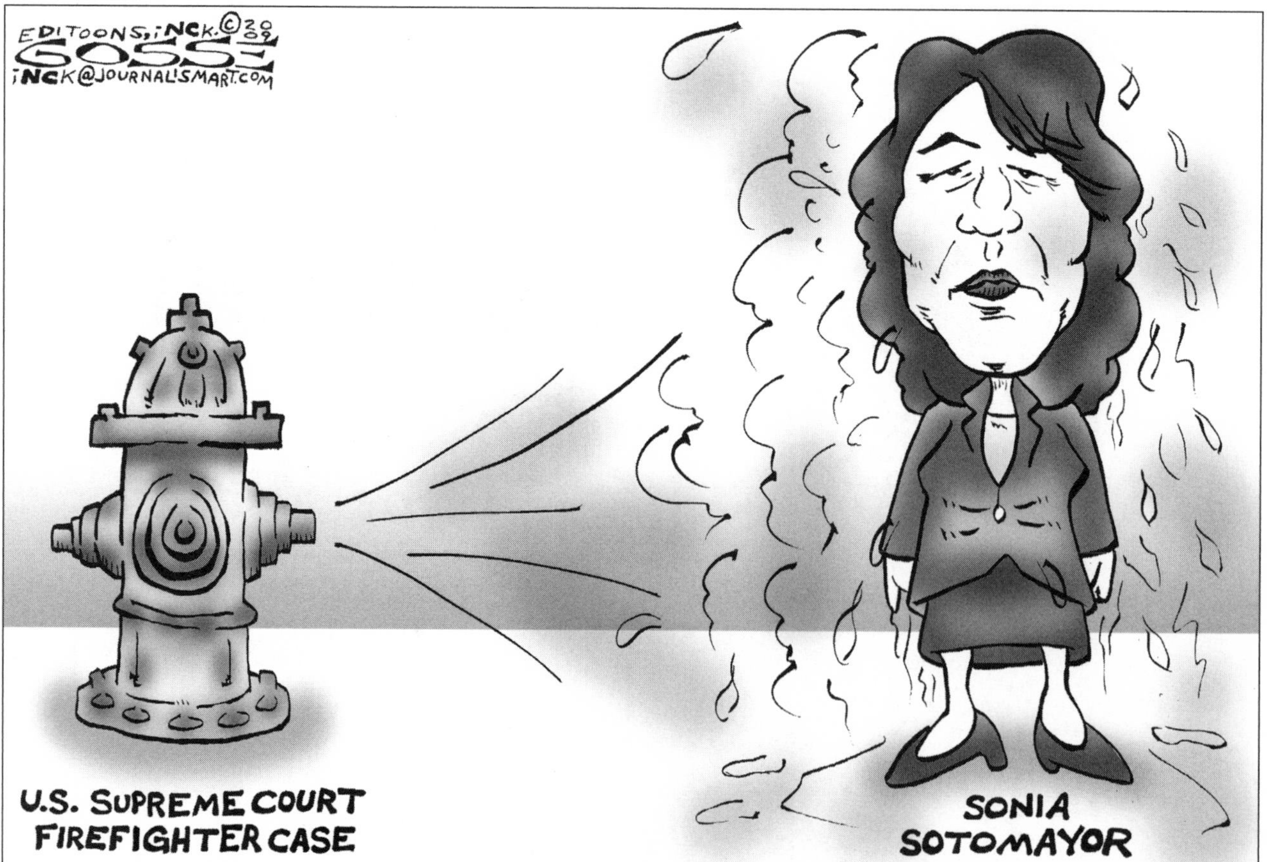

But if judges didn't bring their own experience to cases, wouldn't they all reach the same verdict?

PETER EVANS
Courtesy Islander News (Fla.)

GARY MARKSTEIN
Courtesy Creators News Service

©2009 CREATORS.COM
GARY MARKSTEIN
THEY'RE GETTING DESPERATE TO TRIP HER UP...
I'M THINKING OF A NUMBER BETWEEN ONE AND A HUNDRED...
SENATE
SOTOMAYOR

NEWS ITEM:
Khalid Sheikh Mohammed was waterboarded 183 times.
HUFFAKER
Before
After

SANDY HUFFAKER
Courtesy politicalcartoons.com

CARL MOORE
Courtesy Creators Syndicate

JUSTICE IN THIS DAY AND AGE IS NO LONGER BLIND.
I'M A WOMAN AND A LATINA. WHEN IT COMES TO THE LAW, THAT MATTERS.
www.creators.com
CMoore8949@aol.com
YOU WON'T NEED THIS ANYMORE, HONEY.
©2009 CREATORS SYNDICATE INC.

JEFF KOTERBA
Courtesy Omaha World-Herald

GITMO
KOTERBA
OMAHA WORLD-HERALD

BEATTIE
MADOFF
11695

"He's still inflating his numbers. He's only been here a week."

BRUCE BEATTIE
Courtesy Daytona Beach News-Journal

GARY VARVEL
Courtesy Indianapolis Star

ALL RIGHT, MADOFF! WHERE DID YOU GET THE IDEA OF PAYING EARLY INVESTORS WITH MONEY FROM LATE INVESTORS?
FROM THE SOCIAL SECURITY SYSTEM
GARY VARVEL
THE INDIANAPOLIS STAR
©2008 CREATORS SYND.

©2009 TRIBUNE MEDIA 3-12
LOWE
SOUTH FLORIDA SUN-SENTINEL
MADOFF IN PRISON
I'M SERIOUS... I GAVE HIM THREE BUTTS, AND A MONTH LATER, I GOT A WHOLE CARTON BACK! THE MAN'S A GENIUS!
742

CHAN LOWE
Courtesy South Florida Sun-Sentinel

JOE HELLER
Courtesy Green Bay Press & Gazette

JoeHeller
RETURN BONUSES
RETURN THE MONEY!
BONUSES! FOR WHAT?
CROOKS
GIVE BACK THE BONUSES
AIG
CRIMINALS
AIG
AIG
"HA!... FOOLED THEM... I INVESTED IT ALL WITH BERNIE MADOFF!"

DARREL AKERS
Courtesy Vacaville Reporter (Calif.)

CHUCK LEGGE
Courtesy The Frontiersman

NOT MINE...
Conception
WHEN DOES LIFE BEGIN?
THAT'S ABOVE MY PAY GRADE.
OBAMA

STEVE BREEN
Courtesy San Diego Union-Tribune

CHRYSL FIAT MOTORS
IT DOESN'T FEEL LIKE A CHRYSLER
FIAT
C. Beyl

CHARLES BEYL
Courtesy Lancaster Sunday News (Pa.)

STEVE LINDSTROM
Courtesy Duluth News-Tribune

©lindstrom
DULUTH NEWS TRIBUNE 4-09

PAY INCOME TAX HERE
NATIONAL DEBT

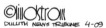

UP UP.. DOWN DOWN.. UP UP... UP UP..
MAKE UP YOUR MIND DUDE!
GASOLINE PRICE
PRODUCERS
MOTORISTS
YOYO... HIS FAVORITE PASTIME
POL GALVEZ © PHILIPPINE NEWS BURLINGAME, CA 8-14-09

POL GALVEZ
Courtesy Philippine News

DAVID HITCH
Courtesy Worcester Telegram & Gazette (Mass.)

WITH A LITTLE PUSH, AMERICA CAN RETURN TO WHAT IT ONCE WAS....
A LAND DOMINATED BY DINOSAURS!
SOCIALISM
PRAVDA
DEATH OF AMERICAN CAPITALISM
HITCH TELEGRAM & GAZETTE

GAMBLE ©2009 THE FLORIDA TIMES-UNION
This new water torture is killing me! Here, scrub my back and I may tell you where I hid the bomb!
al-Qaida Please Knock before entering!
CIA
CIA
JACUZZI-TUB
New Guidelines for interrogating terrorist prisoners!

ED GAMBLE
Courtesy Florida Times-Union

CHARLIE HALL
Courtesy Rhode Island News Group

Cruel, excessive, unnecessary, inhuman and unbearable.
Our torture policy?
No. These hearings.
SHELDON
TORTURE HEARINGS
Charlie Hall

CALIFORNIA ... LAND OF...
...THE GREAT REDWOODS...
...BEAUTIFUL SHORELINES...
...FERTILE FARMLANDS...
3-09 CHUCKASAY
TEMPERATE WEATHER
©2009 CREATORS SYNDICATE, INC. www.creators.com
SILICON VALLEY
HOLLYWOOD
DISNEYLAND
...ENTREPRENEURSHIP...
LIBERAL GOVERNMENT Please Help!
...WORST CREDIT RATING IN THE COUNTRY!

CHUCK ASAY
Courtesy Creators Syndicate

STEPHEN LAIT
Courtesy Oakland Tribune

SO, THE LATEST REPORTS SAY THINGS ARE STARTING TO LOOK UP AROUND HERE...
S. Lait

IN HIS YOUTH, BERNIE MADOFF SOLD INVISIBLE DOGS TO HIS FRIENDS.
VEGOTSKY

KEN VEGOTSKY
Courtesy Bucks County
Courier-Times (Pa.)

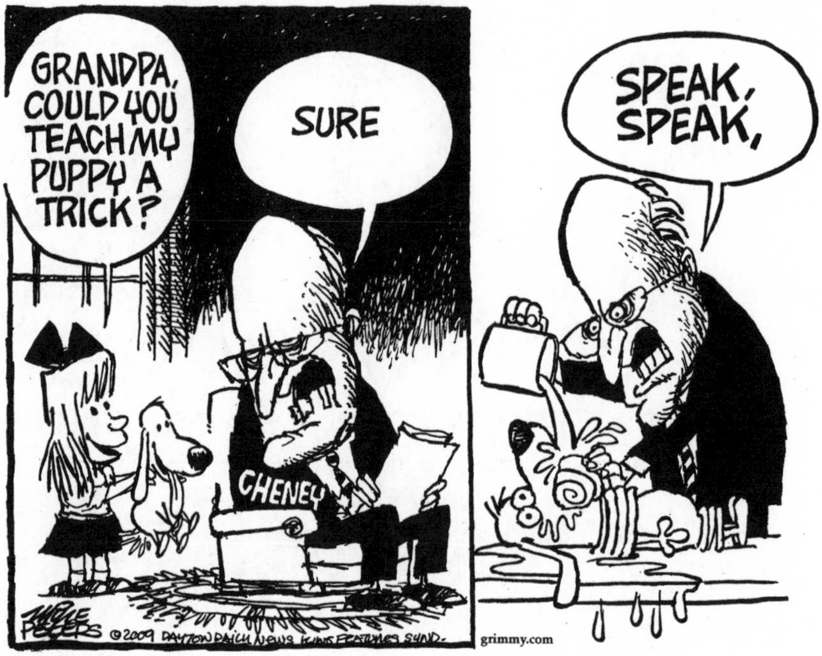
GRANDPA, COULD YOU TEACH MY PUPPY A TRICK?
SURE
SPEAK, SPEAK,
CHENEY
grimmy.com

MIKE PETERS
Courtesy Dayton Daily News

BILL GARNER
Courtesy Creators Syndicate

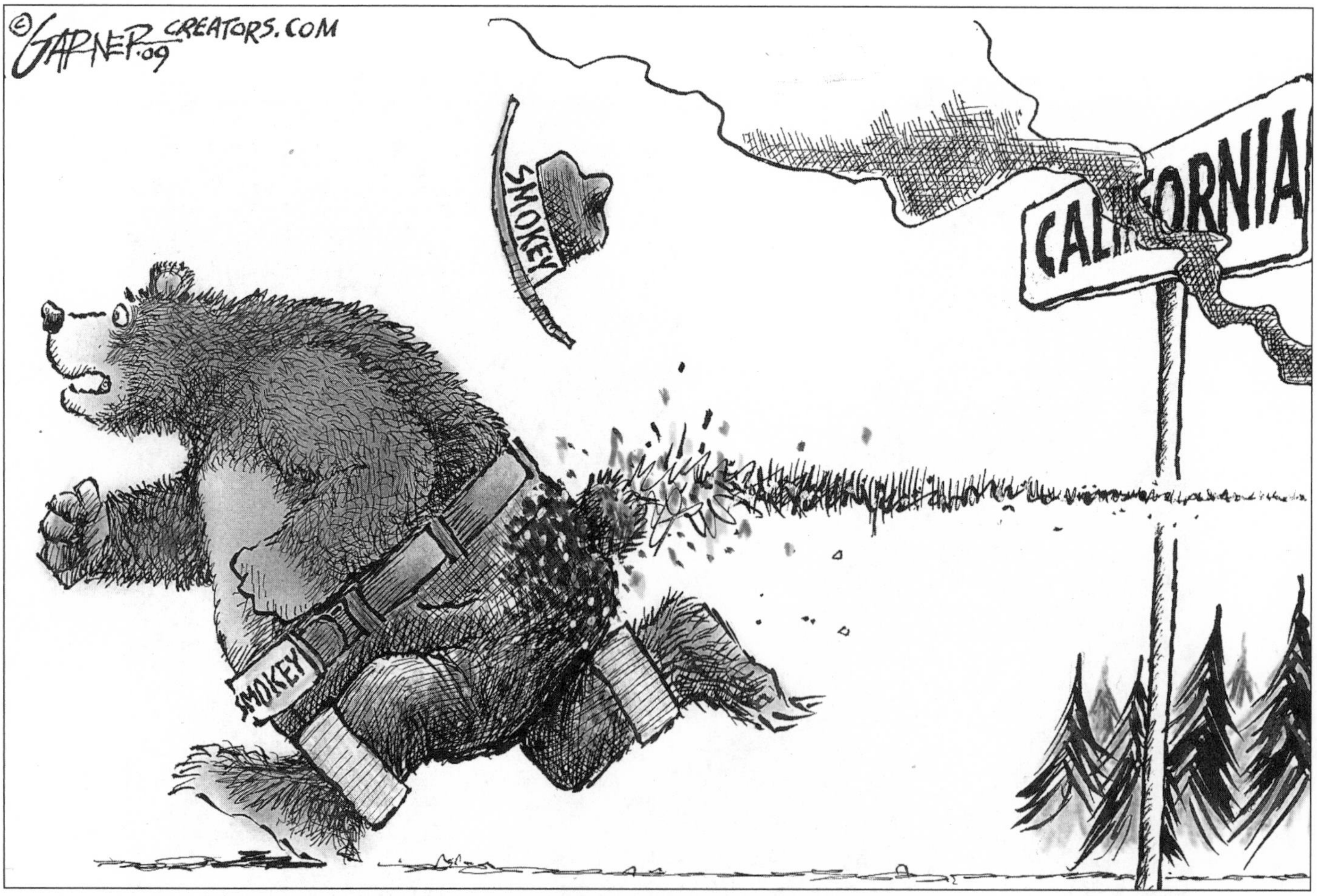
CREATORS.COM
SMOKEY
CALIFORNIA
SMOKEY

ROGER SCHILLERSTROM
Courtesy Crain Communications

KIRK ANDERSON
Courtesy Artizans Entertainment

JIM HUNT
Courtesy Charlotte Post

TIM BENSON
Courtesy Argus Leader (S.D.)

TONY BAYER
Courtesy News-Dispatch (Ind.)

Easy does it flight 1549
US AIRWAYS
MILBRATH ©1.16.09

DEB MILBRATH
Courtesy CNN AAEC

JOHN FULLER
Courtesy Artizans.com

©2009 FULLER
ARTIZANS.COM
"YOU HAVE THE RIGHT TO REMAIN SILENT. ANYTHING YOU SAY CAN AND WILL BE USED AGAINST YOU...."
HE ALREADY KNOWS HIS RIGHTS.
HE'S READING IT TO YOU!
CIA
HOLDER

YOU'RE ONE OF MY ANGELS NOW, FARRAH.
J.R.ROSE! ©2009 BYRD NEWSPAPERS OF VA.
FARRAH FAWCETT
STAR OF TV'S
"CHARLIE'S ANGELS"
1947-2009

J.R. ROSE
Courtesy Byrd Newspapers

MARK STREETER
Courtesy Savannah Morning News

HI! BILLY MAYS HERE!
OH! MR. MAYS! DOES THAT PRODUCT WORK ON REPUTATIONS?
AT LAST! I'M GOING TO MEET CHARLIE!
AND NOW...
TAKE A NUMBER
2
OXI CLEAN
I KNOW, I KNOW, WHEEEERE'S JOHNNY?
OUR LIFE, PASSING BEFORE OUR VERY EYES.
SAVANNAHNOW.COM
MSTREETER SAVANNAH MORNING NEWS © 6.29 09

IT DIDN'T TAKE THE KENNEDYS LONG TO ORGANIZE A TOUCH FOOTBALL GAME, DID IT, PETE?
danielc@knoxnews.com
DANIEL
©NEWS SENTINEL

CHARLIE DANIEL
Courtesy Knoxville News-Sentinel

BOB ENGLEHART
Courtesy Hartford Courant

Englehart ©7/24/09 HARTFORD COURANT.
CBS
THE SECOND MOST TRUSTED MAN IN HEAVEN

THE LEGEND GROWS.
HELLO? NATIONAL ENQUIRER?
HEY! THAT WAS THE LAST BEAR CLAW!
THANKYUHVERMUSH.
JOHN COLE

JOHN COLE
Courtesy Scranton Times-Tribune

J.R. ROSE
Courtesy Byrd Newspapers

JRROSE! ©2009
BYRD NEWSPAPERS
NOW YOU'LL KNOW THE REST OF THE STORY!
PAUL HARVEY

Past Award Winners

PULITZER PRIZE

1922—Rollin Kirby, New York World
1923—No award given
1924—J.N. Darling, New York Herald-Tribune
1925—Rollin Kirby, New York World
1926—D.R. Fitzpatrick, St. Louis Post-Dispatch
1927—Nelson Harding, Brooklyn Eagle
1928—Nelson Harding, Brooklyn Eagle
1929—Rollin Kirby, New York World
1930—Charles Macauley, Brooklyn Eagle
1931—Edmund Duffy, Baltimore Sun
1932—John T. McCutcheon, Chicago Tribune
1933—H.M. Talburt, Washington Daily News
1934—Edmund Duffy, Baltimore Sun
1935—Ross A. Lewis, Milwaukee Journal
1936—No award given
1937—C.D. Batchelor, New York Daily News
1938—Vaughn Shoemaker, Chicago Daily News
1939—Charles G. Werner, Daily Oklahoman
1940—Edmund Duffy, Baltimore Sun
1941—Jacob Burck, Chicago Times
1942—Herbert L. Block, NEA
1943—Jay N. Darling, New York Herald-Tribune
1944—Clifford K. Berryman, Washington Star
1945—Bill Mauldin, United Features Syndicate
1946—Bruce Russell, Los Angeles Times
1947—Vaughn Shoemaker, Chicago Daily News
1948—Reuben L. ("Rube") Goldberg, New York Sun
1949—Lute Pease, Newark Evening News
1950—James T. Berryman, Washington Star
1951—Reginald W. Manning, Arizona Republic
1952—Fred L. Packer, New York Mirror
1953—Edward D. Kuekes, Cleveland Plain Dealer
1954—Herbert L. Block, Washington Post
1955—Daniel R. Fitzpatrick, St. Louis Post-Dispatch
1956—Robert York, Louisville Times
1957—Tom Little, Nashville Tennessean
1958—Bruce M. Shanks, Buffalo Evening News
1959—Bill Mauldin, St. Louis Post-Dispatch
1960—No award given
1961—Carey Orr, Chicago Tribune
1962—Edmund S. Valtman, Hartford Times
1963—Frank Miller, Des Moines Register
1964—Paul Conrad, Denver Post
1965—No award given
1966—Don Wright, Miami News
1967—Patrick B. Oliphant, Denver Post
1968—Eugene Gray Payne, Charlotte Observer
1969—John Fischetti, Chicago Daily News
1970—Thomas F. Darcy, Newsday
1971—Paul Conrad, Los Angeles Times
1972—Jeffrey K. MacNelly, Richmond News Leader
1973—No award given
1974—Paul Szep, Boston Globe
1975—Garry Trudeau, Universal Press Syndicate
1976—Tony Auth, Philadelphia Enquirer
1977—Paul Szep, Boston Globe
1978—Jeff MacNelly, Richmond News Leader
1979—Herbert Block, Washington Post
1980—Don Wright, Miami News
1981—Mike Peters, Dayton Daily News
1982—Ben Sargent, Austin American-Statesman
1983—Dick Locher, Chicago Tribune
1984—Paul Conrad, Los Angeles Times
1985—Jeff MacNelly, Chicago Tribune
1986—Jules Feiffer, Universal Press Syndicate
1987—Berke Breathed, Washington Post Writers Group
1988—Doug Marlette, Atlanta Constitution
1989—Jack Higgins, Chicago Sun-Times
1990—Tom Toles, Buffalo News
1991—Jim Borgman, Cincinnati Enquirer
1992—Signe Wilkinson, Philadelphia Daily News
1993—Steve Benson, Arizona Republic
1994—Michael Ramirez, Memphis Commercial Appeal
1995—Mike Luckovich, Atlanta Constitution
1996—Jim Morin, Miami Herald
1997—Walt Handelsman, New Orleans Times-Picayune
1998—Steve Breen, Asbury Park Press
1999—David Horsey, Seattle Post-Intelligencer
2000—Joel Pett, Lexington Herald-Leader
2001—Ann Telnaes, Tribune Media Services
2002—Clay Bennett, Christian Science Monitor
2003—David Horsey, Seattle Post-Intelligencer
2004—Matt Davies, The Journal News
2005—Nick Anderson, Louisville Courier-Journal
2006—Mike Luckovich, Atlanta Journal-Constitution
2007—Walt Handelsman, Newsday
2008—Michael Ramirez, Investors Business Daily
2009—Steve Breen, San Diego Tribune

SIGMA DELTA CHI AWARD

1942—Jacob Burck, Chicago Times
1943—Charles Werner, Chicago Sun
1944—Henry Barrow, Associated Press
1945—Reuben L. Goldberg, New York Sun
1946—Dorman H. Smith, NEA
1947—Bruce Russell, Los Angeles Times
1948—Herbert Block, Washington Post
1949—Herbert Block, Washington Post
1950—Bruce Russell, Los Angeles Times
1951—Herbert Block, Washington Post and
Bruce Russell, Los Angeles Times
1952—Cecil Jensen, Chicago Daily News
1953—John Fischetti, NEA
1954—Calvin Alley, Memphis Commercial Appeal
1955—John Fischetti, NEA
1956—Herbert Block, Washington Post
1957—Scott Long, Minneapolis Tribune
1958—Clifford H. Baldowski, Atlanta Constitution
1959—Charles G. Brooks, Birmingham News
1960—Dan Dowling, New York Herald-Tribune

PAST AWARD WINNERS

1961—Frank Interlandi, Des Moines Register
1962—Paul Conrad, Denver Post
1963—William Mauldin, Chicago Sun-Times
1964—Charles Bissell, Nashville Tennessean
1965—Roy Justus, Minneapolis Star
1966—Patrick Oliphant, Denver Post
1967—Eugene Payne, Charlotte Observer
1968—Paul Conrad, Los Angeles Times
1969—William Mauldin, Chicago Sun-Times
1970—Paul Conrad, Los Angeles Times
1971—Hugh Haynie, Louisville Courier-Journal
1972—William Mauldin, Chicago Sun-Times
1973—Paul Szep, Boston Globe
1974—Mike Peters, Dayton Daily News
1975—Tony Auth, Philadelphia Enquirer
1976—Paul Szep, Boston Globe
1977—Don Wright, Miami News
1978—Jim Borgman, Cincinnati Enquirer
1979—John P. Trever, Albuquerque Journal
1980—Paul Conrad, Los Angeles Times
1981—Paul Conrad, Los Angeles Times
1982—Dick Locher, Chicago Tribune
1983—Rob Lawlor, Philadelphia Daily News
1984—Mike Lane, Baltimore Evening Sun
1985—Doug Marlette, Charlotte Observer
1986—Mike Keefe, Denver Post
1987—Paul Conrad, Los Angeles Times
1988—Jack Higgins, Chicago Sun-Times
1989—Don Wright, Palm Beach Post
1990—Jeff MacNelly, Chicago Tribune
1991—Walt Handelsman, New Orleans Times-Picayune
1992—Robert Ariail, Columbia State
1993—Herbert Block, Washington Post
1994—Jim Borgman, Cincinnati Enquirer
1995—Michael Ramirez, Memphis Commercial Appeal
1996—Paul Conrad, Los Angeles Times
1997—Michael Ramirez, Los Angeles Times
1998—Jack Higgins, Chicago Sun-Times
1999—Mike Thompson, Detroit Free Press
2000—Nick Anderson, Louisville Courier-Journal
2001—Clay Bennett, Christian Science Monitor
2002—Mike Thompson, Detroit Free Press
2003—Steve Sack, Minneapolis Star-Tribune
2004—John Sherffius, jsherffius@aol.com
2005—Mike Luckovich, Atlanta Journal-Constitution
2006—Mike Lester, Rome News-Tribune
2007—Michael Ramirez, Investors Business Daily
2008—Chris Britt, State Journal-Register

Index of Cartoonists

INDEX OF CARTOONISTS

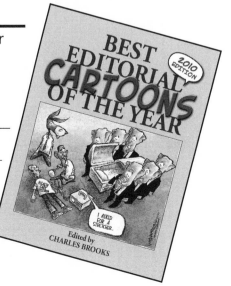

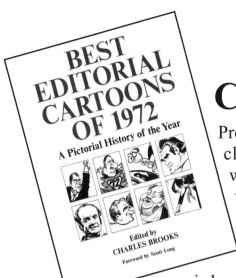